AF564431

ADVANCED COMPUTER APPLICATION IN LIBRARY AND INFORMATION SCIENCE

ADVANCED COMPUTER APPLICATION IN LIBRARY AND INFORMATION SCIENCE

Dr. P. BALASUBRAMANIAN
M.A., M.L.I.Sc., M.Phil., PGDCA, PGDPR, Ph.D.
Deputy Librarian
Manonmaniam Sundaranar University
Tirunelveli (T.N.)

DEEP & DEEP PUBLICATIONS PVT. LTD.
F-159, Rajouri Garden, New Delhi - 110 027

ADVANCED COMPUTER APPLICATION
IN LIBRARY AND INFORMATION SCIENCE

ISBN 978-81-8450-345-6

Typeset by RAHUL COMPOSERS
358, Pocket-B, Phase-2, Sector-16B, Dwarka, New Delhi - 110 075

Printed in India at MAYUR ENTERPRISES
WZ Plot No. 3, Gujjar Market, Tihar Village, New Delhi - 110 018

Published by DEEP & DEEP PUBLICATIONS PVT. LTD.
F-159, Rajouri Garden, New Delhi - 110 027 • Phone : 25435369, 25440916
E-mail : ddpubs@gmail.com • ddpbooks@yahoo.co.in
Showroom :
2/13, Ansari Road, Daryaganj, New Delhi - 110 002 • Telefax : 23245122

Contents

Preface

Today, the information society is passing through various new challenges and opportunities such as librarian professional skills, information management skills and up-to-date subject knowledge.

This book offers the most thorough treatment available on CD Rom. Online access to remote database hosts, Multimedia and Hyper Text, Search Language, Export and Import Data, Library Automation Software Package, etc. in Library and Information Science. For information scientists in software development, programmers, analysis, students, and anyone dealing with issues of information technology in the library or information retrieval, it will be highly informative reference tool.

DR. P. BALASUBRAMANIAN

Acknowledgements

The author feels extremely indebted to Dr. R.T. Sabapathi Mohan, Vice-Chancellor, Manonmaniam Sundaranar University, Tirunelveli and all the teaching and non-teaching staff members of the M.S. University for giving me constant encouragement for writing this book.

I also thank Prof. Dr. A. Rangaswamy, Professor, Management Studies, Infant Jesus College of Engineering, Thoothukudi for help and suggestions.

I would like to thank my beloved wife Mrs. B. Devi and my sweet children who shared my burden and helped me in many ways during the preparation of this book.

I would be a benefit killer if I do not acknowledge the services of Deep & Deep Publications Pvt. Ltd., New Delhi for their efforts in bringing out this book in a record time. Suggestions for further improvement of the book are most welcome.

DR. P. BALASUBRAMANIAN

1

Multimedia

1.1 SUMMARY

As broadband becomes ubiquitous, interactive designers are increasingly called upon to incorporate multiple media and dynamic graphics into their work. Presenting instruction in multiple media can be more effective than doing it through a single medium (such as text), but what is important is combining media effectively, not merely adding media.

Effective multimedia for learning requires carefully combining media in well-reasoned ways that take advantage of each medium's unique characteristics. The most effective multimedia provides learning experiences that mirror real-world experiences and let learners apply the content in various contexts.

1.2 FROM COMPUTER-BASED TRAINING TO MULTIMEDIA

In a previous career, as head of training for a clinical medicine organization, computer-based learning package taught medical terminology to medical assistants, technicians, and transcriptionists. Completely text-based, the program was rather revolutionary for the time. This training was critically important for those who had to know the meaning of terms like "macrovascular" and "macroglossia," and the existence of multiple training options gave them the flexibility to get their training as they needed it.

Jump ahead 15 years to current medical terminology e-learning. Now graphics illustrate each term, audio demonstrates the correct pronunciation, animations allow visualization of different parts of each whole, and video shows everyday use. Learners can make use of electronic flashcards and download print resources for help with studying. The classroom-based course allowed for live interaction. The old computer-based training provided flexibility for training. Multimedia offers the potential to augment learning with a vibrancy that the old computer-based training couldn't easily achieve. For example, multimedia can add clarity through multiple views, as in process guidelines alongside an animation. It can provide depth through additional information channels and resources. It can also add richness and meaning, through video, to show as well as tell. And, if it is not done thoughtfully and well, it can add needless complexity and provoke frustration.

1.3 WELCOME TO MULTIMEDIA LEARNING. WHAT IS MULTIMEDIA?

Definitions of multimedia vary. Richard Mayer, professor of psychology at the University of California, Santa Barbara, defines *multimedia as presentation of content that relies on both text and graphics*. This definition is a good start, but it doesn't provide deep enough insights about the essential factors that can make multimedia effective (or less effective) for learning.

Mao Neo and Ken T.K. Neo, faculty at Multimedia University in Malaysia, extend this definition. They say that multimedia is "*the combination of various digital media types, such as text, images, sound, and video, into an integrated multisensory interactive application or presentation to convey a message or information to an audience.*" This definition appeals because it implies that the combination adds up to more than the elements by themselves, which I believe is the key quality of multimedia when it comes to learning. In any combinations or permutations of common media formats, the whole should be greater than the sum of the parts.

Multimedia certainly has the potential to extend the amount and type of information available to learners. Multimedia can offer layers of beneficial resources, provide gratuitous information leading to frustration and overload, or anything in between. For example, online encyclopedias can provide links to videos and additional articles on specific topics of interest. News stories can reference links to audio commentaries, replays of video footage, and links to websites with additional resources. Online instruction can include explanations, links to resources, simulations, illustrations and photographs, and myriad types of activities that can also include multiple media. Too many resources and media, however, and the benefits get crowded out by the need to figure out what's what.

FIG. 1.0

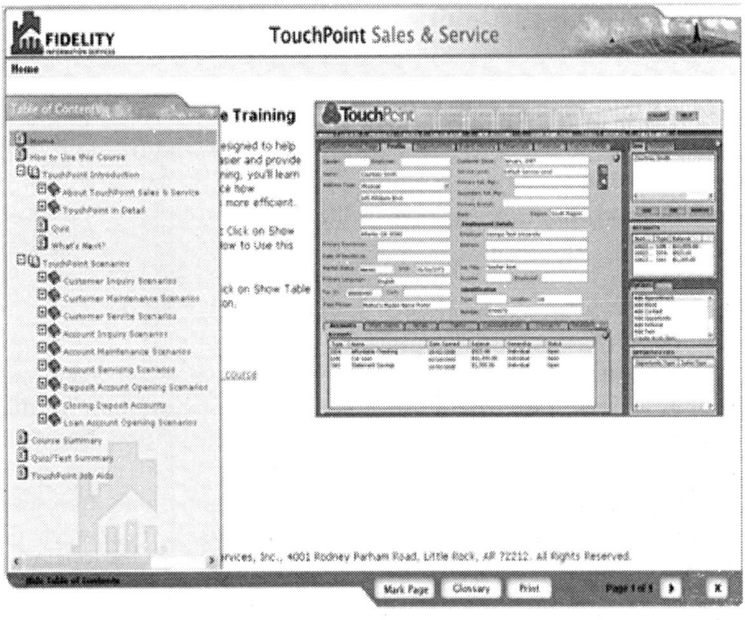

Figure 1.0 shows a screen from a complex application training developed by Learning Peaks. The table of contents (which disappears when not needed, to save screen space) hints at a variety of multimedia devices, including rollovers, animations, simulations, and job aids.

It explains how we process information through two basic channels, verbal and visual. Many people assume that multimedia is obviously better because it uses both channels. Researchers have found that multimedia helps people learn more easily because it appeals more readily to diverse learning preferences. Multiple media can be used to take advantage of the fact that our brains access information in non-linear ways. Although multimedia can provide opportunities for improved learning, it can also be ineffective, even detrimental, when implemented poorly.

1.4 LEARNING AND MULTIMEDIA

Next few sections describes how contemporary learning theory explains the way people learn, how multimedia can augment or detract from learning, research that explains how multimedia impacts learning, design practices that augment learning, and why lack of attention to good design can lead to inferior learning environments.

Before reviewing the research on how multimedia can augment or detract from learning, explore some common notions about how people learn, the complexity of the learning process, and the need to view multimedia research with an eye toward this complexity.

1.5 VIEWS OF LEARNING AND INSTRUCTION

Learning is often viewed as information transfer from one person's head (an instructor or expert) into another's (the learner). Learners are thought to obtain information from an expert and add it to their own memory.

Although this view of learning is widely held, it is too simplistic: it conceives of learners as passive receivers of information and doesn't provide guidance for designing effective learning environments. In fact, designers who hold

Fig. 1.1
Learning as Information Transfer

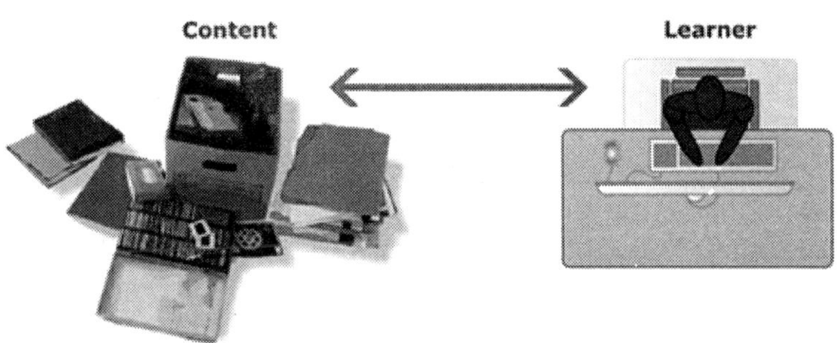

this view of learning often design learning environments that may not include elements critical to effective learning, such as meaningful interaction, feedback, and the ability to learn over time.

A contrasting view is that learning requires people to personally integrate and make sense of new information while they are applying it in their daily lives. In this view, learning

Fig. 1.2
Learning as a complex integrative process transfer

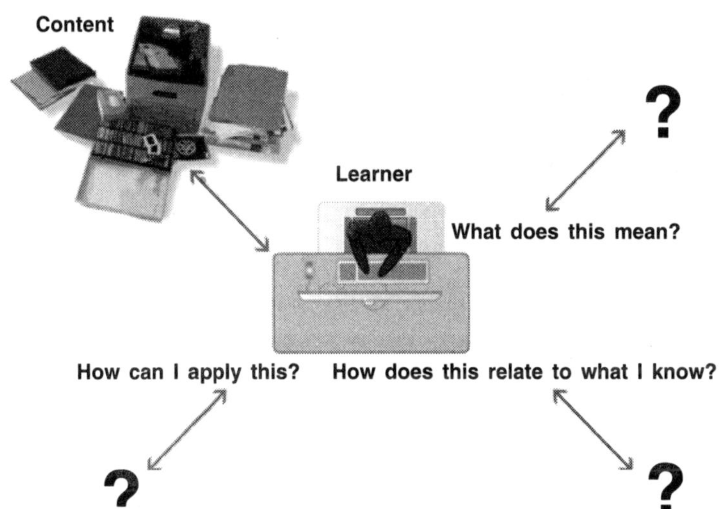

requires struggling to understand how new information meshes with existing knowledge and how to integrate into complex skills and abilities—not just remembering isolated facts or procedures.

Consider the world of difference between merely being able to restate information and the ability to apply the information in the course of living and working. A great deal of instruction is aimed at rote memorization or superficial learning, but that approach doesn't go far enough. Complex skills and abilities that can be used in real life are the true goal of learning, not simply the ability to recall information.

Declarative knowledge is knowing about (the ability to state, list, match, describe, and so on). Procedural knowledge is knowing how (the ability to accomplish complex real-world skills). Copier technicians who can list the parts of the copier have declarative knowledge. Those who know how the parts work together and can use that understanding to troubleshoot a malfunction have procedural knowledge. Declarative knowledge is commonly part of procedural knowledge, but it isn't enough. Too often, instruction is developed at the declarative level, while actual tasks require people to work at a procedural level.

The purpose of effective instruction is to provide formal opportunities for complex skills and abilities—procedural knowledge—to develop. In the transmission model of learning, the point of designing instruction is to present information and then assess whether learners remember it. This model is appropriate when providing information, as opposed to instruction, where no specific skills requirement has been established but not appropriate for instruction. In the construction model of learning, the point of designing instruction is to create opportunities for learners to gain increasingly more complex skills and abilities and then assess whether they apply use the knowledge in real situations.

Contemporary learning theorists such as Spiro, Bereiter, and Brown believe that a key goal of instruction is to provide opportunities for learners to develop mastery in the areas of life they are each involved in. One important step that learners take in developing that mastery is building effective mental models. A mental model is an internal representation of reality. So instruction on how a copier works must help learners internalize how the parts work together so they can operate or fix it, not just match pictures of parts to part names.

Cognitive scientist and consultant Donald Norman describes how accurate mental models help us operate more efficiently and effectively in the world. Helping people form effective mental models has become a primary emphasis in the fields of human-computer interaction and computer usability. Accurate or complete mental models are important in instructional design too, because they are a cornerstone of effective performance.

1.6 BENEFITS OF MULTIMEDIA IN LEARNING

Well-designed multimedia helps learners build more accurate and effective mental models than they do from text alone. Potential benefits of well-designed multimedia, including:

1. Alternative perspectives.
2. Active participation.
3. Accelerated learning.
4. Retention and application of knowledge.
5. Problem-solving and decision-making skills.
6. System understanding.
7. Higher-order thinking.
8. Autonomy and focus.
9. Control over pacing and sequencing of information.
10. Access to support information.

Also describes potential benefits of multimedia. Given that humans possess visual and auditory information processing capabilities, multimedia, it explains, takes advantage of both capabilities at once. In addition, these two channels process information quite differently, so the combination of multiple media is useful in calling on the capabilities of both systems. Meaningful connections between text and graphics potentially allow for deeper understanding and better mental models than from either alone.

FIG. 1.3
Text and Video used Together in Online Sales Skills Training

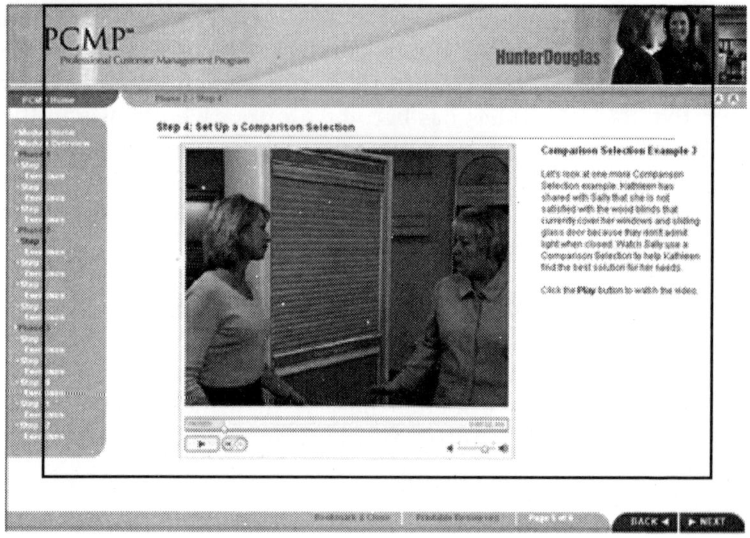

Figure 1.3 shows a screen from sales skills training. In this example, the text on the right briefly describes what the viewer will see in the video. It explains that corresponding text and images should be placed next to each other to improve learning.

How Multimedia Works in Learning

Effectively designed learning environments (including multimedia learning environments) include these four elements:

1. Presentation of information.
2. Guidance about how to proceed.
3. Practice for fluency and retention.
4. Assessment to determine need for remediation and next steps.

Figures 1.4-1.6 show examples of these four elements.

FIG. 1.4
Text and Graphics Used Together to Present Information

FIG. 1.5
Text and Graphics used to Provide Guidance

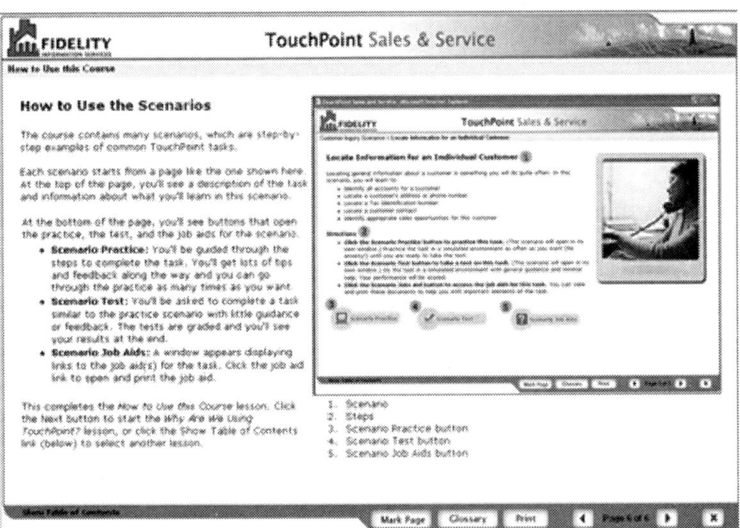

FIG. 1.6
Simulation used in Practice and Assessment

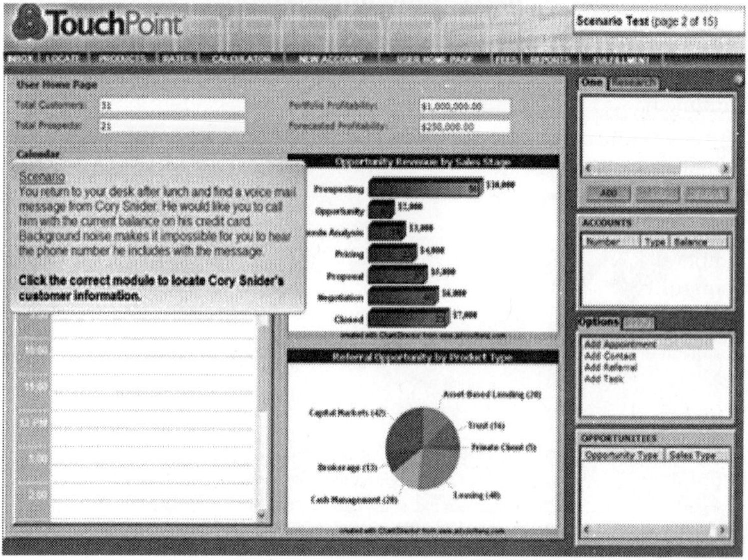

These four elements of a learning environment can be embedded in e-learning or used in a combination of technology-based and non-technology-based instruction, but the environment must include all four elements to be effective. Although most of the elements can be implemented without multimedia, multimedia can make them even more effective and meaningful. Consider earlier example, medical terminology drill-and-practice based on text versus graphics and simulations. Or pages of text hyperlinks versus hyperlinks annotated with pictures and descriptions which help learners determine which links will be most relevant to them. The point is that if the right elements are chosen and combined, they are potentially more compelling and effective.

Research by Mayer is commonly cited to show retention and transfer effects resulting from multimedia when the principles in below are adhered to. These principles stem from cognitive science's understanding of the limitations of working memory and methods for encoding into long-term memory.

TABLE 1.1
Principles that Influence the Effectiveness of Multimedia

Principle	*Description*
Multimedia	Learning from text and graphics is better than from text alone.
Spatial Contiguity	Learning from corresponding text and graphics is better when the corresponding text and graphics are presented near each other.
Temporal Contiguity	Learning from corresponding text and graphics is better when the corresponding text and graphics are presented simultaneously rather than consecutively.
Coherence	Learning is better when there is no superfluous text, graphics, or sound.
Modality	Learning is better with animation and narration than from animation and on-screen text.
Redundancy	Learning is better with animation and narration than from animation, narration, and on-screen text.
Individual Differences	The effects from these principles are stronger for low knowledge and high-spatial learners than for high-knowledge and low-spatial learners.

Multimedia learning is also of interest to people working outside traditional educational fields. Human factors researcher Lawrence Najjar looked at existing research on how multimedia affects learning and found that these practices could be beneficial for learning effectiveness:

1. Select media with the best characteristics for communicating the particular type of information—for example, graphics help people retain spatial information better than text.
2. Use multimedia specifically to support, relate to, or extend learning, not just as embellishment.
3. Present media elements together so that they support each other.
4. Use multimedia that effectively employs verbal and visual processing channels to help learners integrate

content with prior knowledge (this is called elaborative processing).
5. Allow learners to control, manipulate, and explore positively impacts learning and elaborative processing.
6. Use familiar metaphors and analogies, feedback, and personalization to augment motivation.
7. Encourage learners to actively process and integrate rather than receive passively.
8. Match assessments media to presentation of information media.

2.0 DESIGNING MULTIMEDIA APPLICATIONS

In instructional design, the purpose of multimedia isn't just to incorporate multiple media, insert cool effects, or add complexity (which can detract from learning). Use each medium to its advantage and to combine media so that the potential learning is greater and more effective than using single elements alone.

The Table 1.2 shows how different types of media can support different purposes.

TABLE 1.2
Example Media Types and Tools for Various Instructional Purposes

Intructional Purpose	*Media Types and Tools*
(1)	*(2)*
Navigate	Buttons, links, image map, site map, table of contents, nagivation tree, search, help
Explain, document, narrate	Text (explanation, drill-don, instruction manual, text of narration)
Show models, examples, representations	Photo (new copier model). Diagram (how to feed paper into copy machine). Screen capture (menus in an application. Schematic (diagram of audio mixer parts). Process model (flowchart).
Demonstrate qualitative and	Concept map (the Internet, shown as a visual map of related concepts. Chart (organization chart).

(Contd.)

TABLE 1.2 (*Contd.*)

(1)	(2)
quantitative relationships	Graph (correlation between stress and life expectancy).
Show changes over time	Animation (cloud changes before a thunderstorm). Applet (effect of standard deviation on shape of normal curve). Video (showing prospective customer features). Simulation (how alcohol consumption changes reaction time).
Show hidden concepts	Graphical analogies (how compound interest works). Animation (how blood flows into and out of the heart).
Enable direct practice	Simulation (adding and deleting section breaks in a document).

Many of these media types and tools appeared in earlier figures. For example, Figures 1, 3 and 4-6 depict navigation and the use of text and graphics. Figures 6-8 show representations of a real application. Figure 8 shows changes over time and direct practice. Figures 7 and 8, shown next, indicate a process and hidden concepts.

FIG. 1.7
Process Model using Text and Graphics

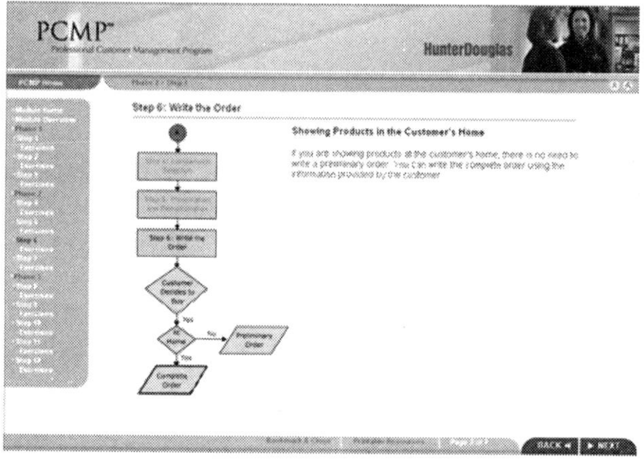

FIG. 1.8
Rollover used to Reveal Hidden Concepts

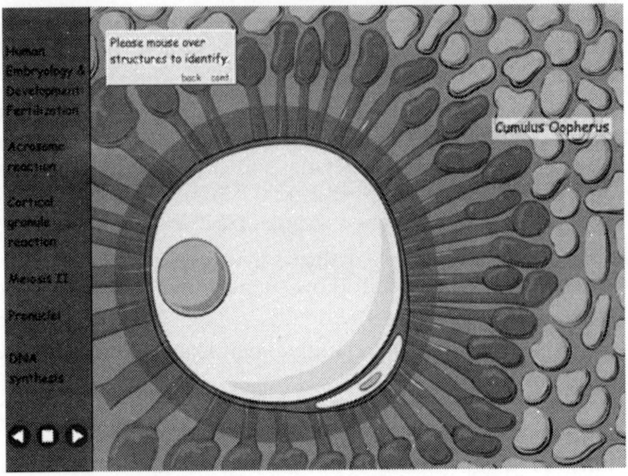

Source : Helen Macfarlane, Medical Illustrator, www.uchsc.edu/ltc/Fertilization.html.

According to theorists like Van Merrienboer, learning environments that are more directed appear to be best for novices, whereas more expert learners tend to prefer less directed approaches. Allowing learners to select the approach that best suits their expertise and learning style (and then change their mind) presents some design (and sometimes resource) challenges but is often needed for a mixed audience.

Well-designed multimedia can enhance motivation, learning, and transfer. The most effective multimedia provides learning experiences that mirror real-world experiences and allow learners to apply what they've learned in various contexts.

3.0 UNIVERSAL MULTIMEDIA ACCESS

Universal Multimedia Access (UMA) is about how users can access the same media resources with different terminal equipment and preferences. For this to be enabled, the media resources have to be adaptable and flexible according to the

FIG 1.9
Universal Multimedia Access

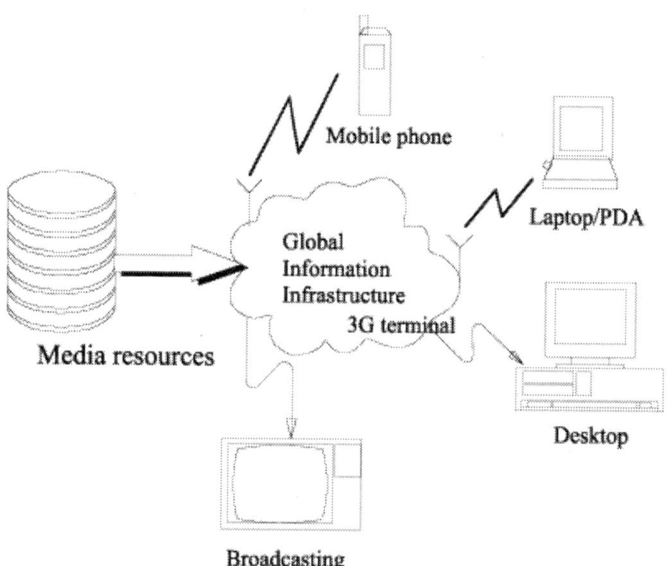

users' needs and capabilities. To accomplish this a media delivery architecture has been developed taking advantage of some of the possibilities in the upcoming Multimedia Framework, MPEG-21. A test bed, used for experimentations and developments of MPEG-21, is under development, which models parts of the UMA concept and MPEG-21. The test bed emulates media resource delivery in a streaming environment, with various terminal and network capabilities. The paper describes the test bed concepts and discusses issues on media representation and presentation relating to a streaming media environment.

Our work has had a strong impact on ISO standardization work such as JPEG2000, MPEG-4, MPEG-7 and MPEG-21. Contributions to JPEG2000 lead to the establishment of a Working Group under the ESPRIT program (EUROSTILL), coordinated by personnel from our department. Further efforts were continued within the ACTS project SPEAR with NTNU as partner. This collaboration has lead to ongoing co-operation with Ericsson Media Lab, EPFL, IMEC, and the University of Wollongong, and is currently kept up through our involvement in MPEG-7 and MPEG-21. At the European level we are part of COST action 276 Information and Knowledge Management for Integrated Media Communications Systems.

Our current project portfolio consists of projects funded by the Norwegian Research Council (UMA-Universal Multimedia Access from Wired and Wireless Systems), NORDUnet2 (Nordic Minister Council, including universal access to the multimedia portal) and industry consortia through Midgard Media Lab.

The Norwegian Research Council funds a PhD based research program focusing on fundamental issues of Universal Multimedia Access. The project involves PhD topics that currently are:

- Adaptive Network architecture and QoS (Dr.Ing.)
- Streaming media and media conversions: Dynamic adjustment of coding rates/active networks (Dr.Ing.)
- Authoring, content production for distributed, layer-structured, scaleable media services (web, TV) (Dr.Art.).

The Nordic Minister Council funds a co-operation between NTNU, Ericsson Media lab, Framkom and SINTEF Telecom and Informatics with the main goals of developing the Communication Infrastructure and streaming media and media conversion for Universal Multimedia Access. In addition there is an educational programme for student and personnel exchange between the partners. Through Midgard Media Lab we are currently establishing a Norwegian initiative in Interactive Advanced Media Technology based upon the Midgard Media Lab framework.

4.0 THE INTERNET AND THE WORLD WIDE WEB

The Internet and the World Wide Web have sent shock Waves through the entire computing industry. They provide the entry into electronic market place of the future. This market place will be based on multimedia network. The superhighway will provide a great opprtunity space for well-designed applications. Good design is needed also for educational multimedia

5.0 CONCLUSION

After experiences the following conclusions have done for corrective maintenance in the manufacturing line:

1. Operator's inspection time is reduced almost to zero, proving the terminal in every machine calls automatically for help when a breakdown is produced.
2. Operator's repairing time is reduced, as far as the system is guiding him through the information shown on the screen, in the operations required to solve the failure.
3. Maintenance dead time does not changes.
4. Maintenance repairing time is dramatically reduced, as the diagnosis is done automatically by the computer, giving an orientation on the possible reasons for the failures. The maintenance force, based on this information can prepare in advance the adequate spare parts and tools required for the job. The interactive, on line and real time information supplied by the computer, save also the time normally needed to consult handbooks, read repair instructions, look for blueprints, and so on.

Regarding the Predictive Maintenance the Following Points must be Emphasised

1. This type of maintenance reduces costs in spare parts and manpower.
2. There is an improvement in the product quality, as far as the machines are kept in better operation conditions, repairing then before they loose their fitness to keep the adequate tolerances.

3. There is also an improvement of the workers safety, avoiding possible accidents, when some machine part becomes suddenly broken in operation.

A good question to ask at this point is "*What are the differences between hypermedia and multimedia?*". Although there is disagreement about these differences, there are two commonly recognized distinctions. Multimedia implies *less user interaction* with the multimedia program or presentation. Multimedia presentations and programs are *sequential* in terms of the *flow of the information*. Hypermedia information spaces are connected by non-linear **links** which a user may follow in any order. Multimedia information spaces are arranged sequentially, with only **one path** through the information provided. Educational television tends to be the prime example of multimedia information.

2

Hypermedia and Hypertext

2.1 MULTIMEDIA, HYPERMEDIA AND HYPERTEXT

Interactive multimedia can be regarded as the superior set of hypermedia.

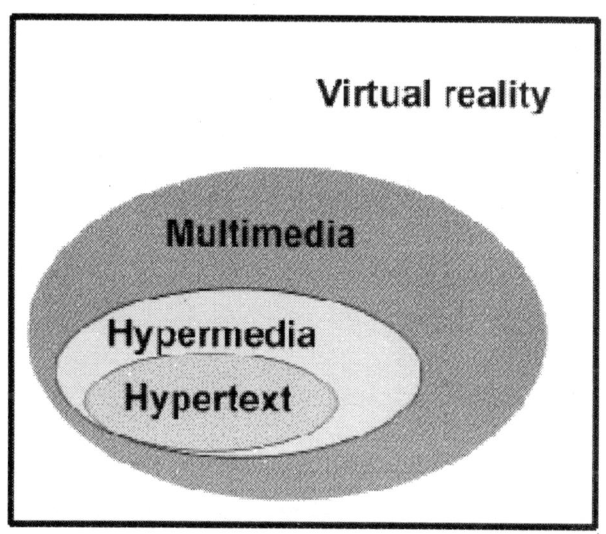

The 'Hyper-hierarchy'

Hypertext can be regarded as a unlined navigator in textual database, where you can directly point at and move between words without linear index or keywords.

Hypermedia is an interactive multimedia document, where you can point at and make links directly between different multimedia objects without using hierarchy index or keywords. Hypermedia is a multimedia with hypertext seeking system.

Multimedia is a computer application that consists of different medias. Multimedia is combined at least of three media's from the following list:

- Text
- Data
- Voice
- Graphics
- Still pictures
- Animation
- Moving pictures

The forms of multimedia application can vary a lot including different PC-, telephone-, fax-, CD-player and camera systems.

Fig. 2.1
HyperText

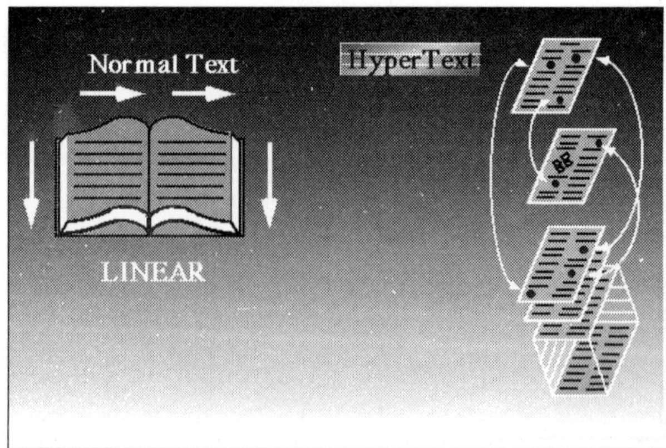

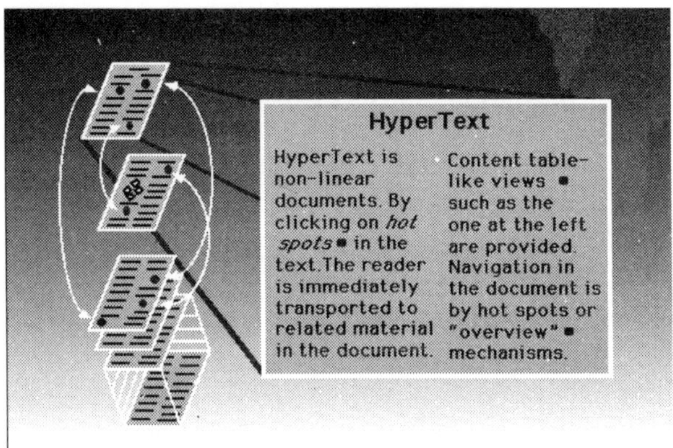

FIG. 2.2
Hyper Media

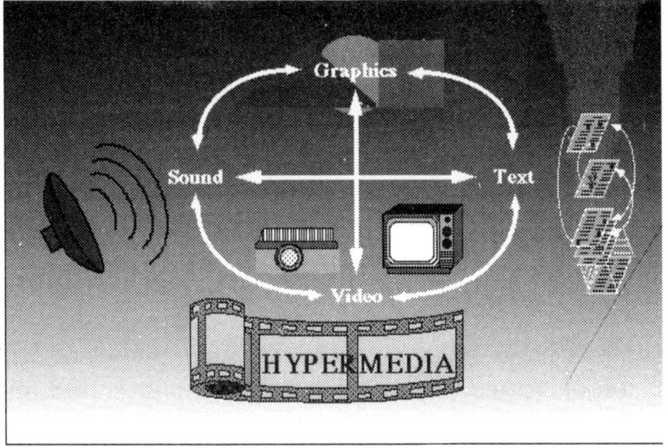

2.2 WHAT IS HYPERTEXT AND HYPERMEDIA?

The operation of the Web relies mainly on **hypertext** as its means of interacting with users. Hypertext is basically the same as regular text-it can be stored, read, searched, or edited with an important exception: hypertext contains connections within the text to other documents.

For instance, suppose you were able to somehow select (with a mouse or with your finger) the word "hypertext" in the sentence before this one. In a hypertext system, you would then have one or more documents related to hypertext appear before you—a history of hypertext, for example, or the Webster's definition of hypertext. These new texts would themselves have links and connections to other documents-continually selecting text would take you on a free-associative tour of information. In this way, hypertext links, called **hyperlinks**, can create a complex virtual web of connections.

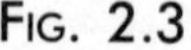
FIG. 2.3

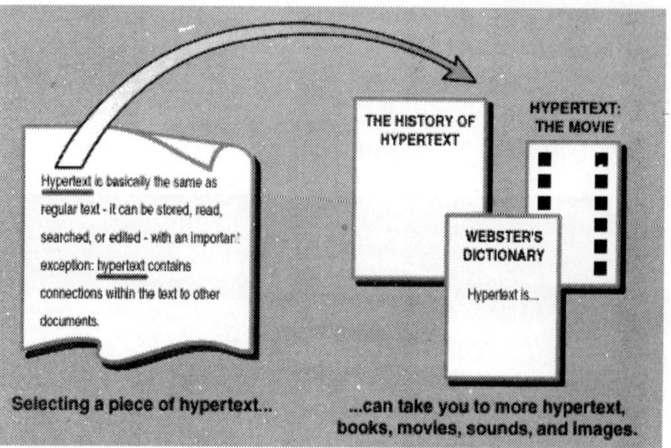

Hypermedia is hypertext with a difference-hypermedia documents contain links not only to other pieces of text, but also to other forms of media-sounds, images, and movies. Images themselves can be selected to link to sounds or documents. Hypermedia simply combines hypertext and multimedia. Here are some simple examples of hypermedia:

- You are reading a text on the Hawaiian language. You select a Hawaiian phrase, then hear the phrase as spoken in the native tongue.
- You are a law student studying the California Revised Statutes. By selecting a passage, you find precedents from a 1920 Supreme Court ruling stored at Cornell. Cross-referenced hyperlinks allow you to

view any one of 520 related cases with audio annotations.

- Looking at a company's floor plan, you are able to select an office by touching a room. The employee's name and picture appears with a list of their current projects.
- You are a scientist doing work on the cooling of steel springs. By selecting text in a research paper, you are able to view a computer-generated movie of a cooling spring. By selecting a button you are able to receive a program which will perform thermodynamic calculations.
- A student reading a digital version of an art magazine can select a work to print or display in full. Rotating movies of sculptures can be viewed. By interactively controlling the movie, the student can zoom in to see more detail.

The Web, although still in its infancy, has already enabled many of these examples. It facilitates the easy exchange of hypermedia through networked environments from anything as small as two Macintoshes connected together to something as large as the global Internet.

2.3 HYPERMEDIA EXAMPLES

Below are examples of different media you can experience via the Web. Your World-Wide Web browser must be properly configured to display these media types.

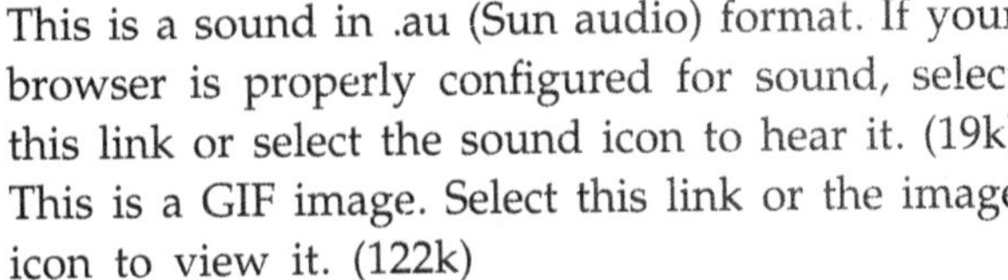

This is a sound in .au (Sun audio) format. If your browser is properly configured for sound, select this link or select the sound icon to hear it. (19k)

This is a GIF image. Select this link or the image icon to view it. (122k)

This is a Macintosh QuickTime movie, with synchronized sound and audio. Select the movie icon to view it. (445k)

Here is the same movie in MPEG format. It has no audio track. (119k)

2.4 WHAT IS HYPERTEXT AND HYPERMEDIA?

We may define hypertext as a text in electronic format making it possible to overcome the limits and bounds of traditional written text on paper. In its simplicity it means that in digital format we may make links into the text (words, sentences) that lead to other pieces of information.

One may argue that in printed text there has always been 'links' such as list of content, indexes, list of references and so one. Right. The difference is that in hypertext, where links are embedded to the text, you may move from one association to another as you read the text. With hypertext, reading comes more a process of "browsing" a text, than traditional linear reading from start to end.

In 1940's an american engineer Vannevar Bush, intorduced the concept of Memex, a device of the future scientist with all books, records and communication integrated to one table. The vision of the Memex was to make the previous collected human knowledge more accessible add secondly to make the scientists work more efficient. The idea of the Memex was presented in Vannevar Bush's 1945 The Atlantic Monthly article *"As We May Think"*.

Memex was thought to be a microfilm-based device with cameras and electromechanical control. The rise of the computer technology made people to think what if the Memex could be implemented in a computer. In the 1960's visionaries, such as Ted Nelson thought that one day with computers we could link all meaningful information to each other, and in this way create a web of all human knowledge and wisdom. His model involved—amongst many other things—the following components: Single sources of documents, sophisticated quoting of source documents, and a royalty scheme to allow both original sources and subsequent collectors/linkers of information to profit from the use of valued information.

Form the late 1960 to today Ted Nelson's main projects has been to developed a software framework that makes possible rich hypertext structures. The system was named to be the Xanadu.

2.5 INFORMATION STORAGE AND RETRIEVAL SYSTEM

Conventional information storage systems are subject to numerous practical constraints such as contiguity in the physical locations of blocks and the requirement that storage blocks be created in advance. Information retrieval in these systems has required the creation of indices, which take a long time to generate, and the structure of these systems makes them prone to deadlock because the indices are updated and the range of exclusion broadened when the referent information is modified. This invention utilizes the random access facilities of semiconductors to achieve high speeds and minimize the maintenance load. This invention introduces location tables and alternate-key tables to replace these indices. It also stores multiple records in a single block and can handle variable-length records and spanned records. The location tables manage the storage blocks. An alternate-key block is made up of a substitute key and its block number and the primary key value, either of which may be used to retrieve a target record by searching this table. Binary search is a well-known high-speed method of querying tables, but other methods may be used as well.

3

Windows

3.1 INTRODUCTION TO COMPUTERS

The computer as we know it is a group of pieces of hardware put together to get a job done faster. To accomplish its various tasks, the computer is made of different parts, each serving a particular purpose almost independent of, or in conjunction with, other parts. You don't necessarily need to know how these parts operate, at least not at this time, but you should be aware of their co-dependence to take advantage of their various characteristics.

FIG 3.1

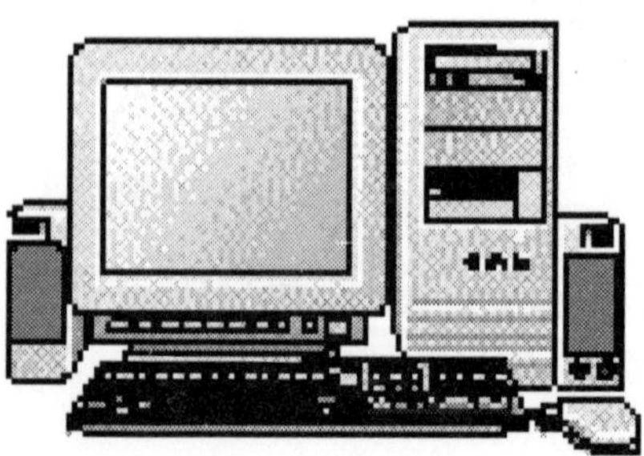

The "computer" is an ensemble of different machines that you will be using to get your job done. A computer is primarily made of the Central Processing Unit (usually referred to as the computer), the monitor, the keyboard, and the mouse. Other pieces of hardware, commonly referred to as peripherals, can enhance or improve your experience with the computer.

The computer works by receiving and giving instructions (in future lessons, we will learn that an instruction or a group of instructions is actually called a program). For example, when you press the power button, you give the instruction to the electricity to "wake" up the computer.

Depending on the computer you are using, when it comes up, it may directly display the desktop or it may ask you to log in. Because there are so many scenarios, we cannot review all of them. If you are using Microsoft Windows 95, 98, Millennium, or XP, the desktop may display once the computer is ready. Some installations of Windows 98 may first display a logon window to you, you can just click OK and you will be fine. Again, there are too many scenarios, we cannot review all of them.

Practical Learning: Starting a Computer

- To turn the computer on, find its Power button and press it when the computer starts, if a dialog asking

Fig. 3.2

you to logon appears, press (**Esc**) on the keyboard. Look at the computer's monitor.

3.1.1 The Central Processing Unit (CPU)

The most important part, also called the Central Processing Unit or CPU, is a box that includes many pieces that are not particularly relevant to us at this time. These pieces, inside of the box, perform the jobs of the computer. One of the assignments of this unit is to join all the other pieces connected to it. Another job of this unit is to perform calculations, exactly the same types of calculations you were performing in primary school, except that this box can handle them very (extremely) fast, so fast that there is no human being who can match that speed. Besides the calculations, this unit also performs other assignments that it receives from various sources including you and the external units that are connected to the CPU.

Fig 3.3

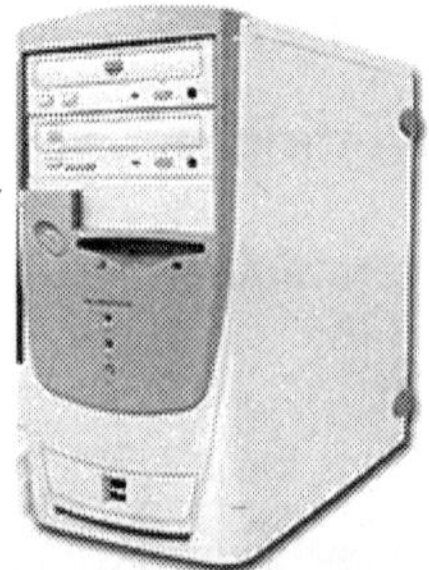

3.2 THE MONITOR

The monitor is the video display you will be looking at, most of the time, to evaluate your work, find out whether the assignments are being carried out satisfactorily. A monitor is largely controlled by some pieces of hardware inside of the computer. But the monitor itself is mainly used to display your work in a graphical setting you can easily interpret. To display what is going on with the computer, the monitor is connected to the computer using a cable. The connection is usually done from the back of both machines.

FIG. 3.4

3.3 THE KEYBOARD

A computer keyboard is a wide object that is equipped with buttons on which there are letters and numbers. To distinguish them from other objects, and to synchronize their names with other objects that use similar settings, such as the piano, the buttons on the keyboard are called keys.

FIG. 3.5

To provide a better management, the keys on a keyboard are divided in sections. This arrangement is by convention so the users would be familiar with them and be able to use any keyboard they come in contact with.

3.4 THE MOUSE

A mouse is an object that is meant to fit the proportions of a hand and is positioned on the table so the user can move it easily. Like the other parts, a mouse is connected to the computer, usually to the back, by a cable. Nowadays, it is not unusual to have a wireless mouse so that it doesn't need a cable.

FIG. 3.6

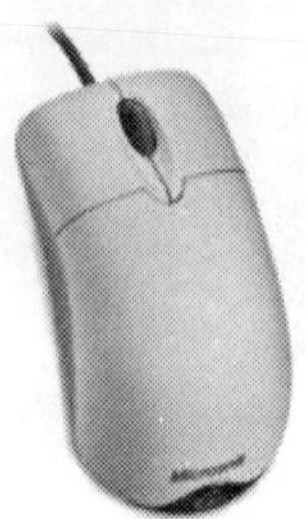

3.5 THE PERIPHERALS

All the parts we have reviewed so far are usually required for the computer to function. Some other parts, not required, can also be connected to the computer to complement it. A peripheral is an object attached to the computer to help it perform some necessary assignments none of the other parts can handle. In most scenarios, no peripheral is required but nowadays, it is unusual for a computer not to have any peripheral at all. The most used peripherals are the printer, a digital camera, a scanner, a projector, an external drive (such as an external CD burner for an old computer), etc.

FIG. 3.7

3.6 THE DESKTOP

A computer is referred to as "desktop" when it is relatively small enough to be positioned on top of a table where a person is working. Such a computer can also be placed on the floor or somewhere under, or aside of, the table, in which case the monitor would be placed on top of the table. This is the most common type of computers used in the office or at home.

A desktop computer is made of different parts that are connected with cables.

3.7 THE LAPTOP

A computer is called laptop when it combines the CPU, the monitor, the keyboard, and the mouse in one unit to be so small that you can carry it on your laps when traveling or commuting. A laptop is also called a notebook. Other parts, such as an external mouse, an external keyboard, or peripherals such as a printer or a projector, can be connected to the laptop. A laptop is only physically smaller than a desktop but, everything considered, it can do anything that a desktop can do

FIG. 3.8

3.8 THE SERVER

A server is a computer that holds information that other computers, called workstations, can retrieve. Such workstations are connected to the server using various means.

This means that they could be connected using cable, wireless connection, etc. Only computers that maintain a type of connection with the server can get the information that is stored in the server.

A server is a computer that holds information that other computers, called workstations, can retrieve. Such workstations are connected to the server using various means. This means that they could be connected using cable, wireless connection, etc. Only computers that maintain a type of connection with the server can get the information that is stored in the server.

3.9 THE MAINFRAME

Mainframe is a computer, usually physically big, that does almost all the jobs for other types of computers that are connected to it. This is a broad definition but other aspects are involved. Like a server, the program (operating system) that runs in the mainframe defines its role.

FIG. 3.9

3.10 INTRODUCTION TO THE DESKTOP

After you have started the computer, the area you are looking at is called the desktop. The desktop is usually different from one computer to another. This is because some items get added as new programs are installed on a computer, and other items get deleted at will. You will learn how to change the way your desktop looks.

The Microsoft Windows desktop is made of various parts. From the upper left to the lower left side of the screen, there are small pictures or images called **icons**. Each one is used to make the computer do something. Some of the most regular icons are:

FIG. 3.10

3.11 MICROSOFT WINDOWS 98, MILLENNIUM, AND 2000

My Computer

My Computer is used to explore the content of your computer and to do other routine things.

Network Neighborhood

You use Network Neighborhood to communicate with other computers if yours is part of a network.

Recycle Bin

When you get rid of (delete) some things on your computer (folders or files), they go to an area called the Recycle Bin where you still have a chance of recalling (retrieving or restoring) them.

Folder

A folder is one of the containers you will be using to store or locate your work.

You will eventually learn how to create and manipulate folders.

The My Computer, Network Neighborhood, and Recycle Bin programs are a kind of folder referred to as System Folder(s), they come standard with your computer. They have fancy (artistic) icons. The folders you create are in yellow color with a small tab and are considered "user created" folders.

3.12 MICROSOFT WINDOWS XP AND WINDOWS SERVER 2003

Apparently because of many complaints of icons that were crowding the desktop, when publishing later Windows, Microsoft gave users the ability to get rid of any icons they didn't like on the screen. Therefore, the only icon that many users now have is Recycle Bin. Here is an example of a Windows Server 2003 desktop that displays only the Recycle Bin icon:

The center and right empty area you are looking at is actually the desktop. Whenever you are asked to use the desktop, the request refers to the whole area you are looking at. But if you are asked to right-click on the desktop, it refers to the empty area of the desktop.

3.13 THE TASKBAR

In the bottom section of the screen, there is (or there may be) a long object. It is called the Taskbar. On the left side of the

taskbar, there is an area with the word Start or. The appearance of this depends on the version of Windows you are using but it plays the exact same role in any version.

On the right side of Start, there is a wide area that is empty when the computer starts. This is actually referred to as the taskbar. As you keep using the computer, this area would be filled with some objects. In some versions (Windows 95, 98, Windows Server 2003), the color of the taskbar may be gray (or Silver). In some other versions (Windows Millennium), the taskbar may be yellowish. In Windows XP, it may be blue.

On the far right side of the taskbar is a section called the tray area. One of the things that this area displays is the current time (as set on your computer).

3.14 COMPUTER SHUT DOWN

After using the computer, you can exit from it, which is also referred to as shutting down the computer. To safely shut down, on the taskbar, you can click Start -> Turn Off Computer.

The steps may be different depending on your operating system.

3.15 FUNDAMENTALS OF APPLICATIONS

3.15.1 The Operating System

The first and most important program of your computer is called an operating system. All the other programs depend on it. Everything that works in your computer is in accordance with the operating system. Since our lessons focus on the popular "personal computer", the operating system we use is called Microsoft Windows.

3.16 COMPUTER PROGRAMS

While the operating system is the central program that is used to coordinate everything in your computer, you will usually not be concerned with the operating system and what it does in your computer. You will use other programs of your computer.

Text Editors: An application is called a text editor when it is used to create and manipulate simple text. All the characters display in the same way. When Microsoft Windows is installed, it also installs the most popular text editor of the operating system called Notepad:

FIG. 3.11

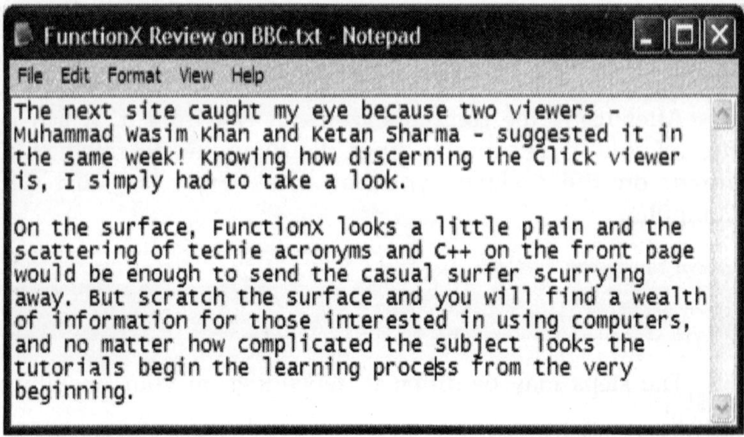

Word Processors: An application is referred to as a word processor when its job is to create text and manipulate it but provide advanced features beyond the capabilities of a text editor. For example, some parts of a document in a word processor may appear in different colors, some sections may display pictures. When Microsoft Windows is installed, it also installs a word processor named WordPad. Word processing assignments are highly demanding nowadays. For this reason, most people and companies purchase commercial word processors published by corporations. Largely the most popular word processor used in Microsoft Windows is Microsoft Word. Other word processors are Sun StartOffice, OpenOffice, or Corel WordPerfect. (See Figure 3.12)

Spreadsheets: A spreadsheet is an application that displays small boxes called cells. Microsoft Windows doesn't install any spreadsheet application. To use such an application, you must install it or have somebody install it for you. The

FIG. 3.12

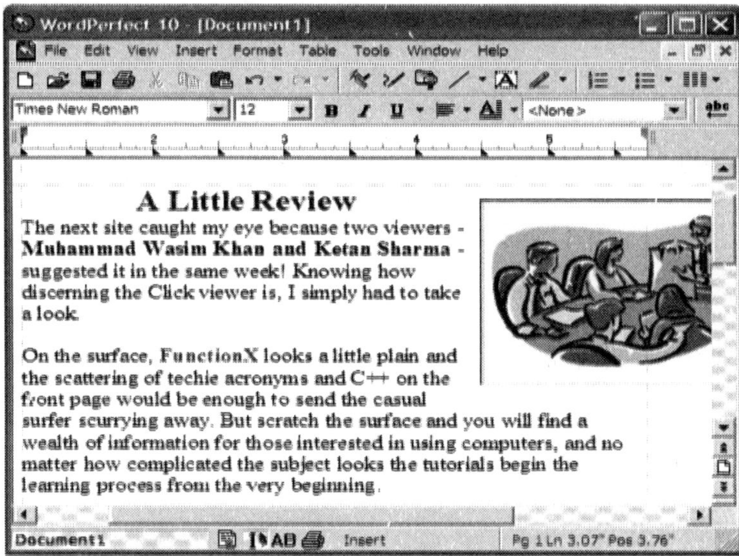

most popular spreadsheet application used in Microsoft Windows is Microsoft Excel:

FIG. 3.13

Microsoft Excel - Persons.xls

File Edit View Insert Format Tools Data Window Help

C14

	A	B	C	D
1	Person ID	First Name	Last Name	Gender
2	1	Elisabeth	Ngouba	Female
3	2	Bertand	Nguyen	Male
4	3	Arnold	Lasante	Male
5	4	Danielle	Mimba	Female
6	6	Armand	Bilonga	
7	7	Germain	Eloundou	
8	8	Anicet	Ngoma	Male
9	9	Anselme	Bibouma	Male
10				

Ready

Other popular spreadsheet applications include Corel Quattro Pro or Sun StarCalc. Other packages include a spreadsheet application. That's the case for OpenOffice or Microsoft Works

Databases: A database application is an environment that is used to create, store, and manipulate series of records. By default, Microsoft Windows doesn't install a database when it is setup. If you need a database application, you may have to purchase one. The most popular database application used in Microsoft Windows is Microsoft Access. Other popular database applications are Corel Paradox or dBase.

Graphics: A graphics application is used to create and manipulate graphics. When Microsoft Windows is installed, it also installs a graphics application named Paint (it used to be called Paintbrush, in previous versions of Microsoft Windows):

FIG. 3.14

Because of the limitations of Paint, people and corporations usually purchase commercial graphics applications. Some of the most popular of them are Adobe Photoshop or Jasc Paint Shop Pro.

3.17 PROGRAM STARTUP

The Start area gives access to most sections or parts of your computer. The Start program on Microsoft Windows XP is a little different than the others but the functionality is the same.

There are various ways you can open a program, sometimes depending on whether you can see it on your desktop. It can also depend on how the program was installed. If a program is available on your desktop, you can double-click it, which would open it.

After you have opened a program, it gets represented on the taskbar so you would know that a program is "running". "Launching" a program means starting it. A program is "running" when it is active on your computer, whether you can see it or it is one of the programs that are activated on your computer.

All of the instructions given in the following lessons are for Microsoft Windows XP.

3.18 PRACTICAL LEARNING: STARTING A PROGRAM

1. To open the My Computer program, on the Taskbar, Click Start and Click My Computer.

Fig. 3.15

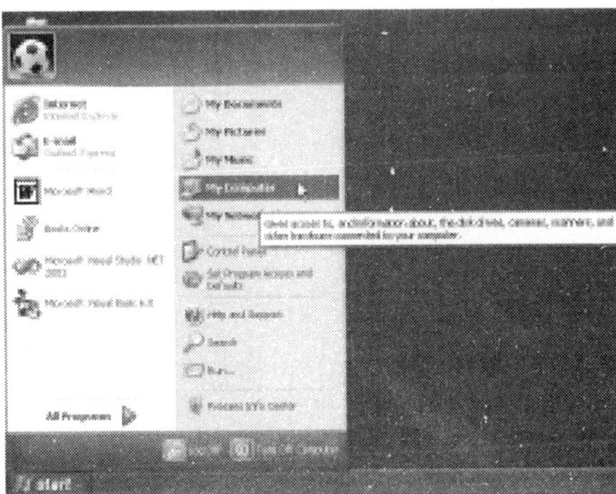

2. Notice that a rectangular object, called a window, displays
3. To close the My Computer window, double-click the small picture on the top-left section of the window 

3.19 WINDOWS MENUS

3.19.1 Introduction

Because there are various assignments you can perform on the computer, the operating system also provides many categories of objects. These objects allow you to perform available actions. The actions you can perform on the computer may depend on the object on which the action is performed and various other options. One of the objects the computer provides is called a menu. To use a menu, you must first know whether and where it is available. We also saw that the menu that appears depended on what you had right-clicked: the Taskbar, an empty area on the desktop, or a picture on the desktop. The menus available on the programs are as varied as the programs themselves are.

Practical Learning : Opening a Menu

1. Start the computer.
2. Click an empty area on the desktop and notice that nothing happens and nothing displays.
3. On the Taskbar, click Start.

FIG. 3.16

4. Notice that a menu appears.
5. Right-click an empty area on the desktop. Notice that a different menu appears.
6. Right-click an empty area on the Taskbar and notice the menu that appears.

Fig. 3.17

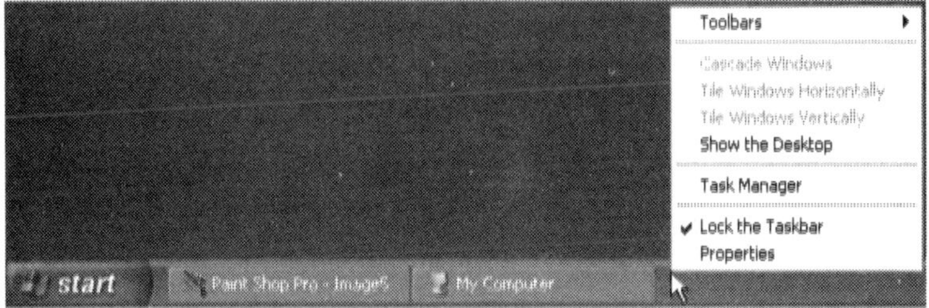

7. Right-click the clock on the right section of the Taskbar and notice the menu that appears:

Fig. 3.18

8. Right-click Recycle Bin and notice the menu that appears.
9. Click an empty area on the desktop. Notice that this dismisses any menu that was opened.

3.20 MAIN MENU DISPLAY

We have just seen that, when you know where a menu is available, to access it, you can just click or right-click the item that holds the menu. How a menu appears can be influenced by the available room. The operating system decides on the availability of room to display the menu. Observe how the same menu is displayed in the following two illustrations:

> If a menu is accessed from the middle to top section of a window, the operating system would display it under the item that was clicked.

Fig. 3.19

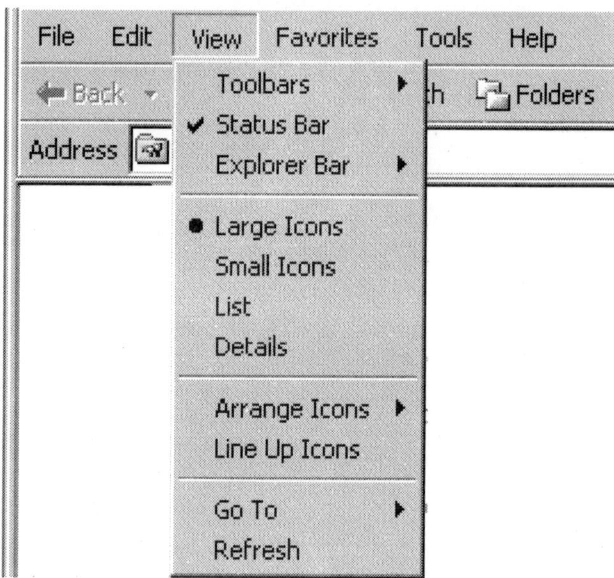

If the menu is being accessed from the bottom section of the screen, the operating system would calculate the available room under the item that was clicked. If there is enough room, the menu would be displayed under the item that was clicked. If there is not enough room, then the operating system would decide to display the menu above the item that was clicked:

FIG. 3.20

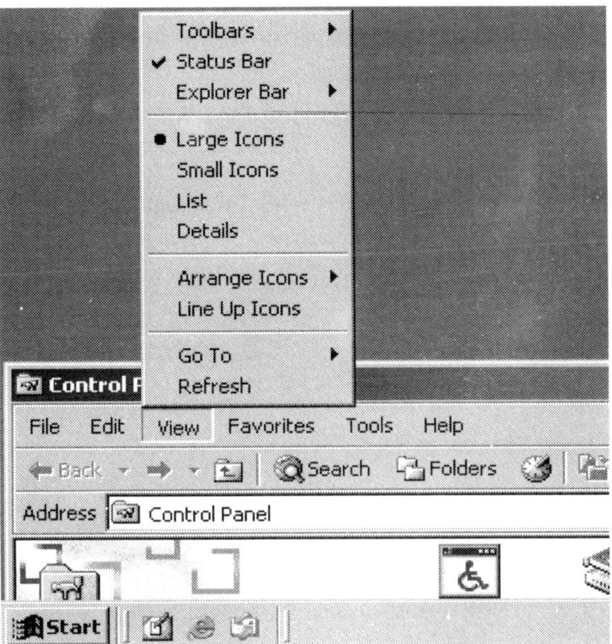

3.21 MENUS CATEGORIES

To diversify the actions that can be performed on a computer, there are six main categories of menus, each of which depends on the person who created the menu:

Stand-Alone Items: The simplest menu item displays a word or a group of words on its line. To use this menu type, you can simply click it. What happens depends on the program. Sometimes, it would appear as if nothing happened, in which case something could have happened behind the scenes. Sometimes nothing at all would happen. Being familiar with the program can give you more information

Disabled Menu Items: If a menu appears gray, this means that the menu is not available at this time. Such a menu

is referred to as disabled. Clicking a disabled menu would not do anything, at all. most of the time, such a menu would require a prerequisite action in order to become available or enabled.

Paste

Ellipsis Menus: A menu with three periods indicates that an intermediary action is required. To use such a menu, click it. Once clicked, sometimes another window would be displayed.

Folder Options...

Check Menus: A menu that appears with a check mark is used as a "witness" of a window object being available or not. This means that, when the check mark is set, the object the menu item refers to is visible. If you click such a menu item, the check mark disappears along with the item it refers to; the menu item is still visible: only its check mark and the item it refers to disappear.

✔ Status Bar

Radio Menus: Some menu items appear in a group of two or more (usually not more than 7). The group is delimited by a horizontal line above the top menu item and another horizontal line below the bottom object.

At any time, one of the menu items has a big round dot on its left side. This dot is called a radio button. The item that is currently active has the radio button and the other menu items don't. If you click an item other than the one with the radio button, the dot moves to the item you clicked and the previous item looses the radio button.

This type of menu is used when the programmer wants only one item of the group to indicate which item of a category is active.

Fig. 3.21

Arrow Menus: When a menu appears with an arrow, this means that the menu item holds its own list, called a submenu. Again, this design depends on the person who created the menu and is not subject to any preconceived rule. To access the menu item, simply position the mouse cursor on the menu item that has the arrow. How the submenu appears may depend on the section of the screen from where the menu is being accessed. The operating system decides how to display this submenu based on the available room.

If the menu with arrow is accessed from the upper-left section of a window, the submenu would display on the right side of the menu and under the arrow:

Fig. 3.22

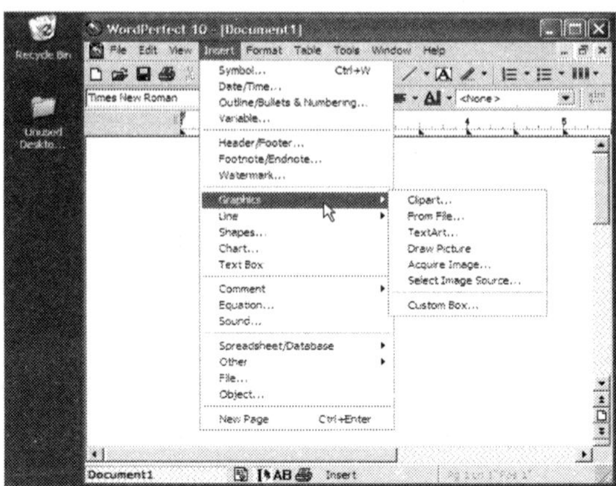

If the menu is accessed from the upper-right section of the window, the operating system would check if there is enough room to display the submenu to the right and under the arrow. If there is enough room, the menu would be displayed as above. If there not enough room, then the submenu would be display on the left side of the menu and under the arrow.

FIG. 3.23

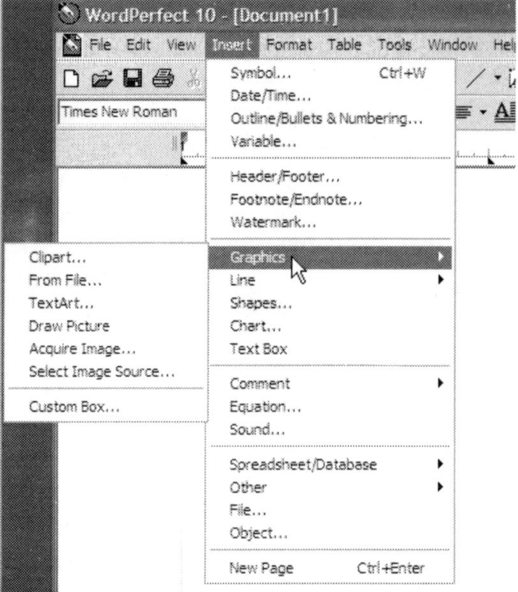

If the menu is accessed from the lower-left section of the window, the operating system would check if there is enough room on the right side of the menu and under the menu with arrow. If there is enough room, the submenu would display under the arrow.

If there is not enough room under the menu, the submenu would be displayed on the right side of the menu but above the arrow.

FIG. 3.24

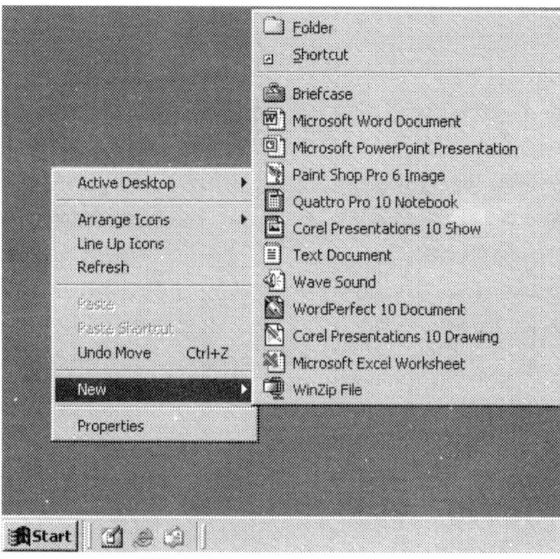

If the menu is being accessed from the lower-right section of the screen, if there is enough room on the right side of the menu, the submenu would be displayed on the right side of the menu but above the arrow.

FIG. 3.25

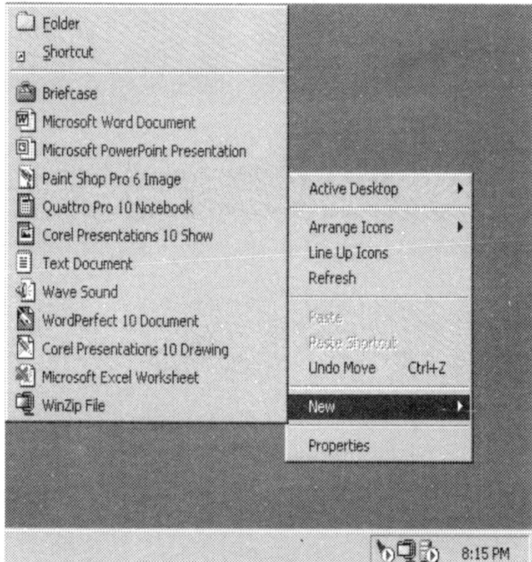

If there is not enough room on the right side of the arrow, the submenu would be displayed on the left side of the menu but above the arrow.

Practical Learning: Using Categories of Menus

1. On the Taskbar, click Start.
2. To dismiss the menu, click an empty area on the desktop.
3. On the Taskbar, right-click Start and notice that a different type of menu appears.
4. On the menu, click Explore:

Fig. 3.26

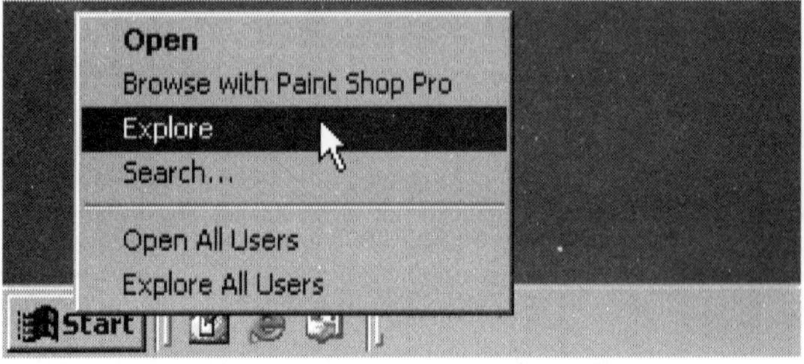

5. To close the window, double-click the small picture on its top-left corner
6. On the Taskbar, click Start, position the mouse cursor on Programs (if you are using Microsoft Windows XP, position the mouse on All Programs).
7. Notice that many names of programs appear.
8. To dismiss the menu, click Start again.
9. On the desktop, right-click an empty area (not any button).
10. Position the mouse on Arrange Icons, and click by Name. (See Figure 3.27)
11. Notice the items on the desktop have been ordered by name.

Fig. 3.27

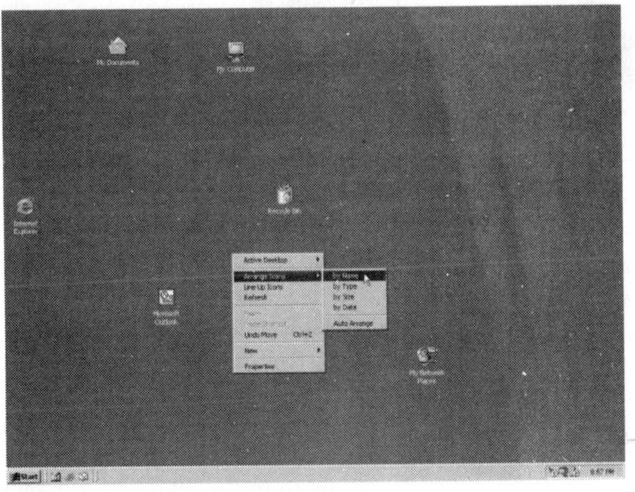

3.22 MAIN AND CONTEXT-SENSITIVE MENUS

We have seen that a menu on the same object can be different depending on what item you click to access such a menu. Based on this, a menu that appears when you simply click an object is considered the regular menu of the object, and it is simply called the menu. Sometimes when you click or even right-click an object, a menu might not appear. On the other hand, if a menu appears when you right-click an item or an area of a window, this menu is referred to as the context-sensitive menu.

Most applications display a menu in their top section. On this site, such a menu will be referred to as the Main Menu. The main menu displays columns of menus, each column is represented by a word (sometimes it will be more than one word for a menu item). To use this main menu, you can click a word. This causes a list of menu items to display. There are no strict rules (only suggestions) on what items must appear under what word. The person who creates an application also decides on the menu columns, their items, and their roles.

After clicking a menu column, if you find the item you are looking for, you can click it. If you don't see the item you are looking for and you want to check another column, you have two options. You can simply move the mouse to another menu column of your choice. You can also click the menu item you had opened, then click the new column you desire. If you still don't see what you are looking for, you can dismiss the menu.

There are various ways you can dismiss the menu if it is opened. If you click an item in the list of the displayed column, the menu would retract and close itself. If you have opened a menu but don't want to use it anymore, you can click one of the menu items on top. You can also click anywhere other than the opened menu; this also closes the menu. We will also learn how to close the menu using the keyboard.

If a menu appears when you right-click an item, we will call it the context-sensitive menu. When necessary, you will be directed when to use the main menu or the context-sensitive menu.

3.23 WINDOW REPRESENTATION

3.23.1 Introduction

In order to use an object, you must be aware of it. A window makes itself known using two types of representations: an icon and/or a frame.

3.23.2 The Icon Representing a Window

An icon is a picture used to identify a program or another type of object on the computer. As such, the small pictures that appear on the computer desktop are called icons. Besides the desktop, there are many other places where you will see icons when using the computer.

There are two entities that mainly need to interact with icons:

- As a person using the computer, icons allow you to familiarize with the various programs that are installed in a computer. Every application or every category of application has its own icon. This is easily possible because every person who creates an application has the possibility of providing a special icon for that particular application.

- The operating system also has an interior mechanism to identify an icon or a type of icon and associate it with a particular application or a series of applications of the same type.

Microsoft Windows ships with various icons for its own use. For example, every version of Microsoft Windows ships with a special icon for the My Computer program. There is also a special icon for Recycle Bin, etc.

The sizes of icons are standardized and they should not have just any random dimensions. For example, the icons on the desktop are 32x32 pixels. Sometimes, the icons display in a 16x16 dimension.

Practical Learning: Using Icons

1. Start the computer.
2. To see some icons, on the Taskbar, click Start, position the mouse on (All) Programs.
3. Notice that each program is represented by an icon. Notice also that all menu items that have an arrow use the same type of icon used on Accessories. These are called Program Groups.
4. Position the mouse on Accessories and click Windows Explorer. If you are using Windows 98 and you don't see Windows Explorer, look for it in the list under Accessories (not in the arrow menu from Accessories).
5. On the left side of the window, click My Computer. Notice that it has a small icon on its left.
6. On the main menu of the window, click View -> Icons or View -> Large Icons.
7. Notice that the icons on the right side are big. (See Figure 3.28)
8. Right-click an empty area on the right side, position the mouse on View and click List or click Small Icons. (See Figure 3.29)
9. Notice that the icon on the upper-left section of the

FIG. 3.28

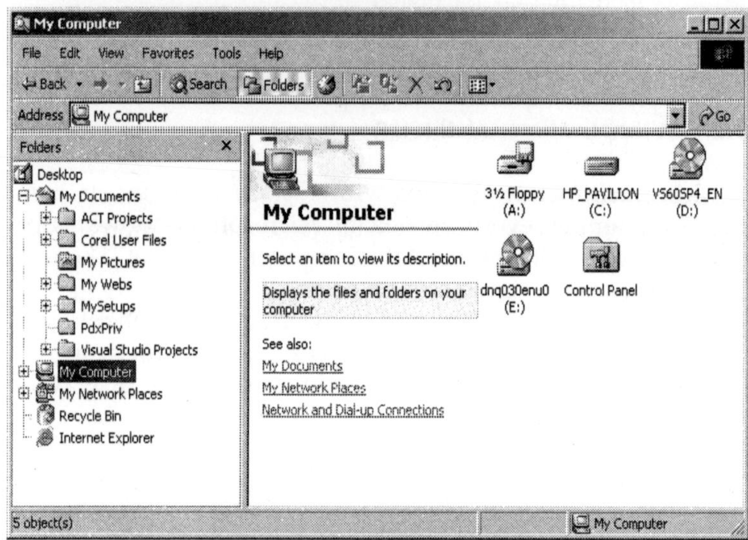

FIG. 3.29

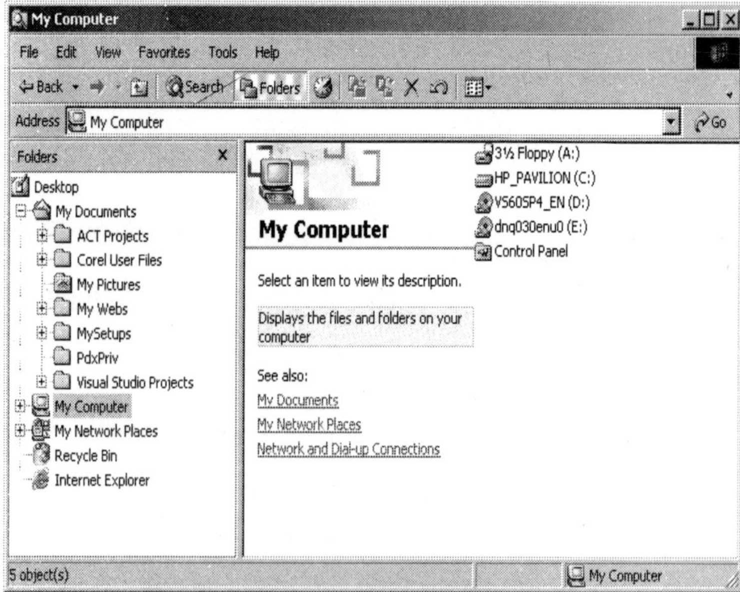

window, the icons in the left frame, and those in the right frame are the same size

10. To close the window, on the main menu, click File -> Close.

3.24 WINDOWS CONTROLS

3.24.1 Introduction

To make your interaction with the computer more useful, the Microsoft Windows operating systems provide various types of objects also called windows. Some of these windows are standard and can be seen in many applications. Some other windows can appear more complex as the companies that develop them are creative. Regardless, there are basic functionalities that most windows share. Therefore, before starting to get creative with the computer, you should be familiar with what is already available and get used to as many features as possible with the computer.

The major categories of what you and I call windows come in four families: A dialog box, a Single Document Interface (SDI), a Multiple Document Interface (MDI), and the Windows Controls. To explore them, we will not necessarily proceed in that order. But we will eventually see all of them as we move along.

3.24.2 Control's Focus

The focus is a visual aspect that indicates that a control is ready to receive input from you. Various controls have different ways of expressing that they have received focus.

Button-based controls indicate that they have focus by drawing a dotted rectangle around their text. In the following picture, the button on the right has focus:

FIG. 3.30

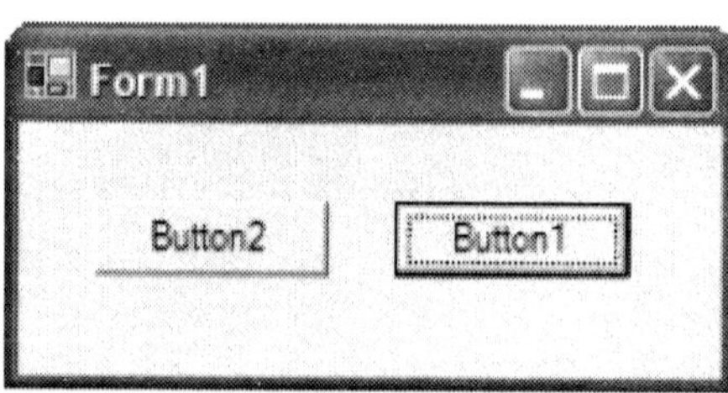

A text-based control indicates that it has focus by displaying a blinking cursor. A list-based control indicates that it has focus when one of its items has a surrounding dotted rectangle:

FIG. 3.31

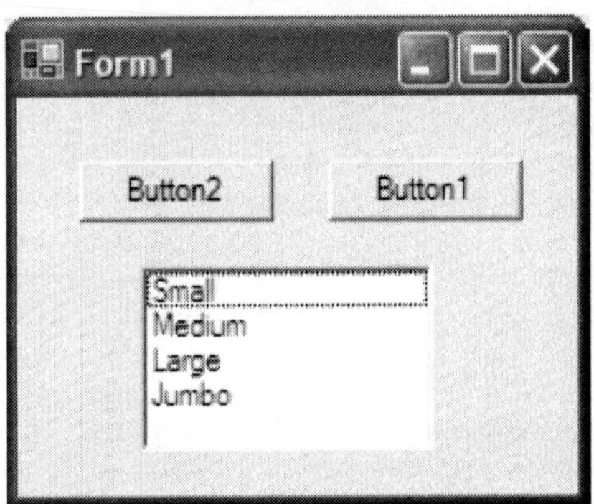

To give focus to a control, you can click it. Alternatively, if the focus is already on one of the controls, to give focus to a particular control, you can press Tab continuously until the control shows that it has focus. On a browser, if you press Tab continuously, the focus would move from one link or control to another. This means that a link on a web page can receive focus as if it were a control.

3.24.3 Dialog Boxes

A Dialog Box is a square or rectangular window whose main role is to carry, hold, or host, other windows. By itself, a dialog box means nothing. The other objects displayed on it define its role. Like a dialog box, the types of objects whose role is to host other objects are called containers. Therefore, the primary role of a dialog box is as a container.

Displaying a dialog box depends on the instructions you are given.

A dialog box is made of two main sections. On top, it displays a title bar. The left side of the title bar displays a sentence as the title of the dialog box. This group of words is also called the caption. Each dialog box is called by its title. Therefore, if the title displays Employees Registration, then the dialog box is called the Employees Registration Dialog Box. We will use the same naming convention in our lessons.

On the right section of the title bar, a normal dialog box would display only the system Close button or By convention, a dialog box cannot be minimized or maximized. Therefore, it doesn't have those system buttons.

Sometimes, a dialog box will have a button with a question mark. This is called the Help button. A dialog box equipped with this button indicates that you can get quick help on the items displayed on the dialog box. While the behaviors of the system buttons seen in previous lessons are defined and controlled by the operating system, the person who creates a dialog box and equip it with the Help button also defines what happens if you click that Help button.

The main section of a dialog box can be referred to as its body (programmers call it the Client Area). This is the area where the objects the dialog box is hosting are positioned. There is no predefined directive nor a restriction on what types of objects a dialog box can hold. It is left to the programmer to decide.

3.24.4 Command Buttons

A command button, commonly called a button, is a rectangular object that displays a word or a group of words, expecting you to make a decision. You make your decision by clicking the button. The button is usually placed on a dialog box but it can also be placed on another type of container.

As far as you (the user) are (is) concerned, the most important characteristic of a button is the word or sentence it displays. This is called the caption. The most basic common button you will encounter has a caption of OK. The buttons available on a dialog box, including their behaviors, once again, depend on the programmer.

In many circumstances, the buttons come as a group. For example, you may have a dialog box with OK and Cancel buttons. Many dialog boxes have an OK and a Cancel buttons. Sometimes, they will have more than one button.

Whenever a button has an OK and a Cancel buttons, clicking the OK button tells the computer that "I accept the changes I made" or "I agree with the changes made", or simply, "I agree". Clicking the Cancel button tells the computer that "Never mind", or "No, cancel your suggestion", or "Dismiss what I did". The documentation of the dialog box you are using should give you enough information about the buttons on the dialog box.

3.25 TEXT BOXES

A text box is a window that is used to display text or to receive text from you. The type of text it displays or the type of text you are asked to provide depends on the application or the situation.

Some text boxes' are used only to display text. Either you cannot change the text or only an intermediary action can make it possible to change the text. Some other text boxes would require you to enter text. If you don't, something bad might happen. Some text boxes would display text already, giving you the chance to change the text or to accept the one suggested to you.

In all or most circumstances, you will be informed about the text box and what you are supposed to do with it.

3.26 THE SCROLL BARS

A scroll bar is an object that is used to navigate from one end of a window content to another. There are two types of scroll bar: vertical and horizontal.

A vertical scroll bar allows you to navigate up and down to display a hidden section of a document. A horizontal scroll bar allows you to navigate left and right on the document.

To scroll a bar, click the arrow of the section you want to display.

3.27 LIST BOXES

A list box is a rectangular control that displays a list of

items. If you see the item that is convenient to the issue at hand, then you can click it. Once an item is clicked, it becomes highlighted, indicating that the item has been selected. If you want to change your choice, you can click another item. Clicking another item deselects the previous item and selects the new one.

Depending on how a list box was configured, you may be able to select more than one item from the list. This is because, as set by the creator of the control, some list boxes allow only one selection while others could let you select as many objects as you want.

To select one item from the list, click it.

To select more than one item, click one of those you need. Press and hold Ctrl. Then click each of the desired items from the list. While making these selections, if you click an item by mistake, to deselect it, click it again and the item would appear "normal". After making the desired selection, release Ctrl. The selected items would be highlighted.

To select items in a range, for example, if a list has ten items and you want to select from the 3rd to the 7th item, click either the top item of your desired range, or click the last item of the range you want to select. Press and hold Shift. Then click the item at the other end of the range and release Shift.

3.28 THE DROP DOWN COMBO BOX

One of the types of combo boxes is referred to as Drop Down. This control is made of a text box on the left side and

FIG. 3.32

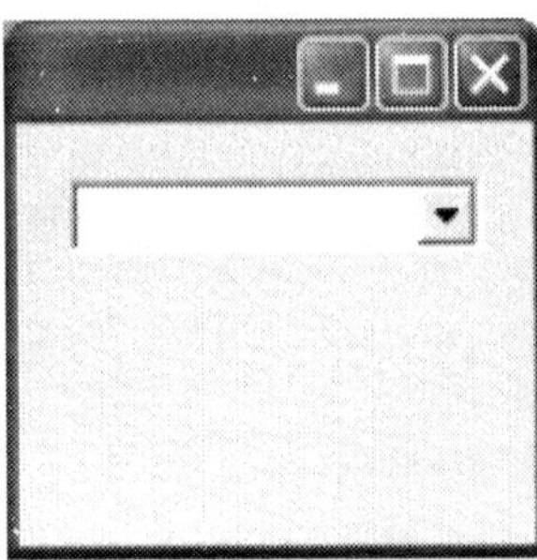

a down-pointing arrowed button on the right side. Depending on how the control was created, when it comes up, it may not display anything.

To use the combo box, you can click its down pointing arrow. If you click that arrow, a list would appear (or expand):

Fig. 3.33

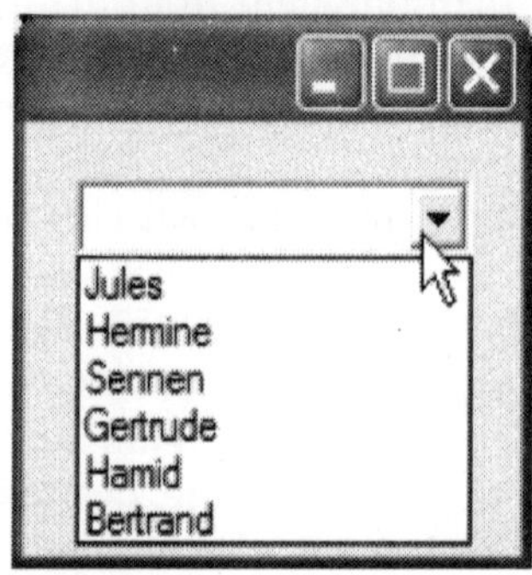

3.29 TOOLBARS

A toolbar provides a quick access to the most frequently used actions performed using the menu. A toolbar offers these items as buttons. For WordPad, the top toolbar is called the Standard toolbar:

Each toolbar b button is used to perform a different and particular action. When you position the mouse on top of a button, a tool tip appears, letting you know what the button is used for.

WordPad is equipped with a second toolbar called the Formatting toolbar. Besides the usual buttons, a toolbar can offer many other windows controls, some of which we will explorer later.

3.30 STATUS BARS

The Status Bar helps as a guide to the users of an application. In a typical application, it displays small sentences that further explain the role of a particular button or an action that you are about to perform. The messages that appear on the Status Bar vary from one application to another and depend on the position of the mouse on an application.

3.31 THE SINGLE DOCUMENT INTERFACE

WordPad is a Single Document Interface application, which means it allows you to work on only one opened document at a time. On top of most or all of Windows applications, there is the title bar:

Document - WordPad

On the left side of the title bar, there is an icon that identifies the application you are using. This icon is called the system icon. Every application that looks like WordPad is equipped with this type of icon but the icons are different from one application to another. This is because the person who creates the application also designs the icon that goes with it. The system has its own menu called the system menu. To access this menu, simply click the system icon.

On the right side of the icon, the name of the file is followed by the name of the application you are using, in this case WordPad. This sequence is not the same on all applications. Again, it depends on the application and how the programmer decided to make it appear.

3.32 TEXT EDITING AND PROCESSING

3.32.1 The Clipboard—Introduction

The Clipboard is an area of the computer that behaves like a short (human) memory with its strengths and weaknesses.

Advantages

- Compared to human memory, the clipboard can be given information, it keeps it, and doesn't forget
- The clipboard memory is very huge, so much that it can contain almost anything from one character to a whole book, from a simple piece of text to a highly rich picture of millions of colors.
- Any (type of) application, by default, can use and access the clipboard.

Disadvantages

- The regular clipboard of Microsoft Windows can hold only one unit of information. For example, it can hold only one picture at a time, or only one character, or only one paragraph of text. If you change its information, it looses the previous information and replaces it with the new one
- The clipboard looses the information it holds when the computer is turned off Like the human memory, you don't see the computer clipboard: You just know that it is there. There are two main ways you use the clipboard: to put information in it or to retrieve the information it holds.

3.33 TEXT PROCESSING

3.33.1 Text Processing and Characters

Character addition usually consists of adding a character at the end of a word. Normally, this means that you would type a new character to the right side of an existing word. Character inserting consists of entering a new character anywhere inside of a word. Character deletion consists of removing an existing character from text.

3.34 TEXT PROCESSING AND WORDS

Word addition consists of adding a word at the end of a

paragraph but before the last period. Word insertion consists of adding a new word somewhere inside of a paragraph.

3.35 TEXT PROCESSING AND PARAGRAPHS

Paragraph addition consists of adding a new paragraph at the end of the document. Paragraph insertion consists of creating a new paragraph somewhere inside of the document. The new paragraph can be made of text or you may be asked to create an empty space between two paragraphs.

3.36 TEXT FORMATTING

3.36.1 Fundamentals of Text Formatting

As mentioned already, what you need to format text depends on the application you are using. With WordPad, the most fundamental used to format text is the Formatting toolbar:

The Formatting toolbar is equipped with three combo boxes and a few buttons. Like any toolbar, to know what a button is used for, position the mouse on top of it, a tool tip will appear.

3.37 FONTS

3.37.1 Introduction

A font is a series of characters designed to draw symbols or readable letters. This design can be made by an individual or a company. After the design has been made, it is electronically made available to individual or companies that can use it to draw characters. Based on this, there are various ways you can get a font in order to it. Because it is designed, a font usually belongs to the designer or is copyrighted. This means that you should have some concerned with getting or using a font.

3.37.2 Getting a Font

There are various ways you can get a font to your computer. When Microsoft Windows gets installed, it also installs various fonts that would be used in the various applications and can be used you. The list of fonts of a computer can be seen from the Fonts icon of Control Panel.

Besides the default fonts, you can install new fonts to your computer. If you install some commercial applications such as Corel WordPerfect or Microsoft Office, it may install various fonts it would use. Once such fonts have been installed, they can be used by other applications of the same computer, not just the application that installed or needs them.

Various web sites also sell or distribute fonts, free or for a fee.

You can purchase a graphics package, such as Corel Gallery, that also includes fonts. Once you get and install such a package, you would have the option to also install or add fonts.

3.38 FILE PROCESSING

3.38.1 File Processing Media

File processing consists of creating something on a computer and keeping it. The thing you keep is called information or datum. The plural of datum is data. In some cases, the word data can be used in both singular and plural forms. There are various issues related and different techniques used to keep data.

A medium is an object used to hold information in a computer. The plural of medium is media. There are various kinds of them.

Internal Hard Drives
External Hard Drives
Internal CD Drives
External CD Drives
Internal DVD Drives
External DVD Drives
Flash Drives

3.39 A DOCUMENT

When you start entering text in a text editor or a word processor, you are said to create, or work on, a document. If you start drawing shapes or manipulating pictures in a graphics application, you are said to work on a document. If you start entering numbers and performing calculations in a spreadsheet, you are said to work on a document.

3.40 FOLDERS

3.40.1 Directories

To make it possible to easily recognize its information in a computer that runs Microsoft Windows, a drive, such as those we have reviewed above, uses some units. The primary unit is called a directory. In Windows Explorer or My Computer, a directory is represented by a letter. Here are examples:

FIG. 3.34

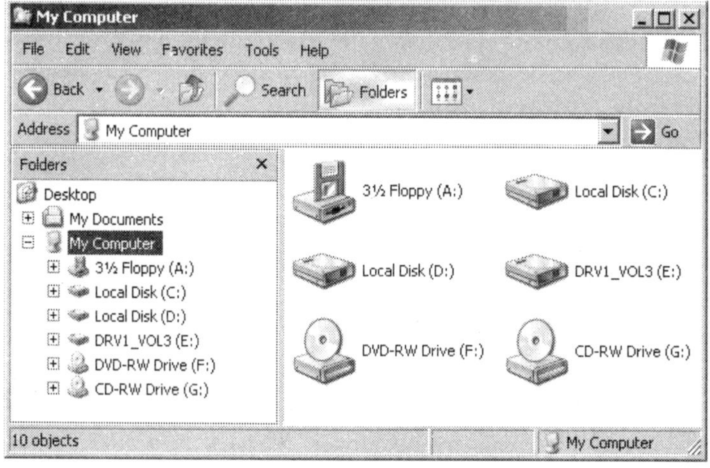

When (the disc of) a drive is created, it doesn't contain directories. This is because the manufacturer doesn't decide how and on what type of computer the drive will be used. When a drive is installed on a computer, the operating system decides about the drive, creates it as a directory and assign a letter to it. You can store a document on a drive but this is not recommended.

3.40.2 Creating a Folder

To better organize the information that it contains, one or more units can be created on a drive. Each unit is called a folder. When (the disc of) a drive is created, it doesn't contain folders. When the operating system is installed, it creates a few folders. You also can create a folder and you have many alternatives.

When it comes to folders, a drive is called the root folder or simply, the root. To create a folder in the root, in Windows Explorer or My Computer:

- In the left frame, click the drive. On the main menu, click File -> New -> Folder and give it a name.
- In the left frame, click the drive. In the right frame, right-click a white empty area, position the mouse on New and click Folder. Then give it a name.

You can also create a folder inside of another. The folder that will contain the new one is referred to as the parent folder. The other will be referred to as a child folder. To create a folder in another folder, in Windows Explorer or My Computer:

- In the left frame, expand the drive by clicking its + button. Under the drive, click the folder name. If the new folder will be created inside of another folder that itself has a parent, expand it also and click the parent folder. On the main menu, click File -> New -> Folder and give it a name.
- In the left frame, click the drive and click the parent folder. In the right frame, right-click the parent folder, position the mouse on New and click Folder, then give it a name.

You can also create a folder when saving a file. To do this, in the dialog box that comes up, click the Create New Folder button and give it a name.

MS Office

4.0 OVERVIEW

MS OFFICE involves the basics of the essential Microsoft Office applications: Microsoft Word, Excel, FrontPage, Publisher, and PowerPoint.

4.1 INTRODUCTION TO MS-WORD

Let us consider an office scene. Many letters are typed in the office. The officer dictates a letter. The typist first types a draft copy of the letter. The officer goes through it to check mistakes regarding spelling errors, missing words, etc. and suggests corrections. The typist changes the letter as suggested by the officer. This is a simple example of word processing.

There are many software packages to do the job of word processing. Some of them work in DOS environment. Examples are WordStar, Word Perfect and Professional Write. But in these days working in WINDOWS is becoming more and more popular. So let us consider software for word processing which works in WINDOWS. Our choice is MS WORD because it is the most popular software in these days.

MS WORD is a part of the bigger package called MS OFFICE, which can do much more than word processing. In fact when you open up MS OFFICE you will find four main components in it. They are MS WORD (for word processing), MS EXCEL (for spreadsheet), MS ACCESS (for database management) and MS POWERPOINT (for presentation purposes). However, we will limit ourselves to MS WORD only in this lesson.

4.2 OBJECTIVES

After going through this lesson you should be in a position to:

- start the MS WORD package
- be familiar with the MS WORD screen
- advantages and Features of Word Processing
- some common Word Processing Packages
- how to invoke MS Word
- learn the capabilities of MS Word

4.3 WHAT IS WORD-PROCESSING?

Word Processor is a Software package that enables you to create, edit, print and save documents for future retrieval and reference. Creating a document involves typing by using a keyboard and saving it. Editing a document involves correcting the spelling mistakes, if any, deleting or moving words sentences or paragraphs.

(a) Advantages of Word Processing

One of the main advantages of a word processor over a conventional typewriter is that a word processor enables you to make changes to a document without retyping the entire document.

(b) Features of Word Processing

Most Word Processor available today allows more than just creating and editing documents. They have wide range of other tools and functions, which are used in formatting the documents. The following are the main features of a Word Processor :

(i) Text is typing into the computer, which allows alterations to be made easily.
(ii) Words and sentences can be inserted, amended or deleted.
(iii) Paragraphs or text can be copied/moved throughout the document.
(iv) Margins and page length can be adjusted as desired.
(v) Spelling can be checked and modified through the spell check facility.
(vi) Multiple document/files can be merged.
(vii) Multiple copies of letters can be generated with different addresses through the mail-merge facility.

(c) Some Common Word Processing Packages

The followings are examples of some popular word processor available :

- Softword
- WordStar
- Word perfect
- Microsoft word

4.4 IMPORTANT FEATURES OF MS-WORD

Ms-Word not only supports word processing features but also DTP features. Some of the important features of MS Word are listed below:

(i) Using word you can create the document and edit them later, as and when required, by adding more text, modifying the existing text, deleting/moving some part of it.
(ii) Changing the size of the margins can reformat complete document or part of text.
(iii) Font size and type of fonts can also be changed. Page numbers and Header and Footer can be included.

(iv) Spelling can be checked and correction can be made automatically in the entire document. Word count and other statistics can be generated.

(v) Text can be formatted in columnar style as we see in the newspaper. Text boxes can be made.

(vi) Tables can be made and included in the text.

(vii) Word also allows the user to mix the graphical pictures with the text. Graphical pictures can either be created in word itself or can be imported from outside like from Clip Art Gallery.

(viii) Word also provides the mail-merge facility.

(ix) Word also has the facility of macros. Macros can be either attached to some function/special keys or to a tool bar or to a menu.

(x) It also provides online help of any option.

4.5 GETTING STARTED WITH MS WORD

We have already told you that for working in Ms-Word you should be familiar with WINDOWS. If you have not covered WINDOWS so far then read that first and then go through MS WORD. By now you must be aware of the fact that a software package is improved from time to time. These improvements are sold in the market as new *versions* of the same software. Thus you will find many versions of MS WORD being used in different offices. In this lesson we will cover the version MS WORD 97, which is latest in the market and contain many improvements over the older versions. However, you do not have to worry if you have an older version such as WORD 6.0 or WORD 95. All the commands available in these older versions are also available in WORD 97 and they are compatible.

While working in MS WORD you have to work with a **mouse.** Also one can work, to some extent, through the keyboard. The use of mouse is simpler as it is fully menu driven. In MS WORD every command is available in the form of 'icons'.

You can go inside MS WORD by the following way.

FIG. 4.1

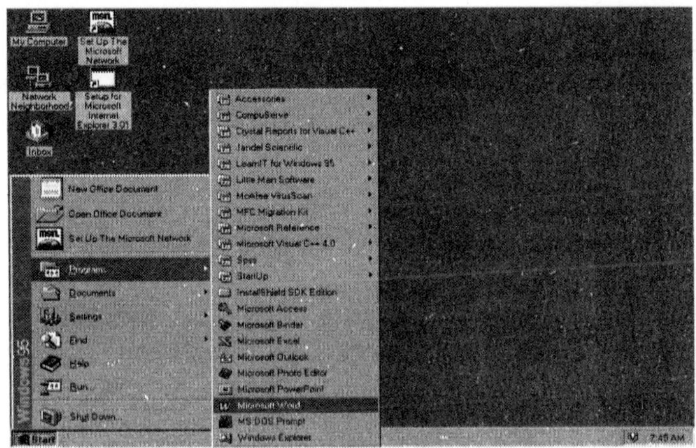

1. Take the mouse pointer to START button on the task bar. Click the left mouse button. The monitor will show like as follows:
2. Move the pointer to **programs**. You will notice another menu coming up to the right.
3. In that menu identify where **Microsoft word** is placed. Move the cursor horizontally to come out of **programs**.
4. Move into the rectangular area meant for **Microsoft word.** Click the left mouse button there. The computer will start MS WORD. You will find the screen as follows :

FIG. 4.2

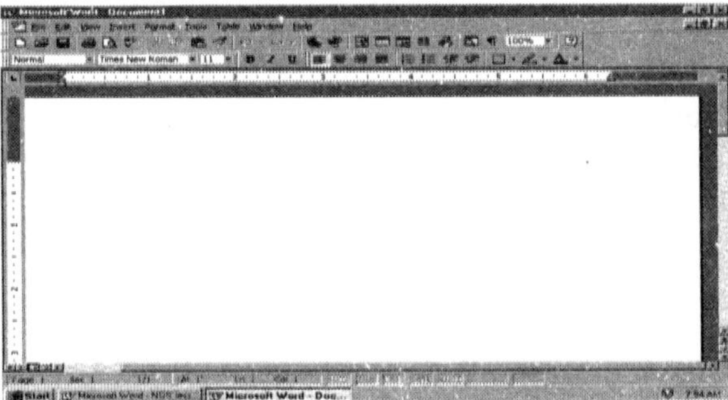

Let us discuss the important components of the screen.

(a) Title Bar

The title bar displays the name of the currently active word document. Like other WINDOWS applications, it can be used to alter the size and location of the word window.

(b) Tool Bars

Word has a number of tool bars that help you perform task faster and with great ease. Two of the most commonly tool bars are the formatting tool bar and the standard tool bar. These two toolbars are displayed just below the title bar. At any point of time any tool bar can be made ON or OFF through the tool bar option of View Menu.

(c) Ruler Bar

The Ruler Bar allows you to format the vertical alignment of text in a document.

(d) Status Bar

The Status Bar displays information about the currently active document. This includes the page number that you are working, the column and line number of the cursor position and so on.

(e) Scroll Bar

The Scroll Bar helps you scroll the content or body of document. You can do so by moving the elevator button along the scroll bar, or by click in on the buttons with the arrow marked on them to move up and down and left and right of a page.

(f) Workspace

The Workspace is the area in the document window were you enter/type the text of your document.

(g) Main Menu

The Word main menu is displayed at the top of the screen as shown in the Figure. The main menu further displays a sub menu. Some of the options are highlighted options and some of them appear as faded options. At any time, only highlighted options can be executed, faded options are not applicable. Infect if the option is faded you will not be able to choose it. You may not that any option faded under present situation may become highlighted under different situations.

4.6 MAIN MENU OPTIONS

The overall functions of all the items of main menu are explained below.

(a) File

You can perform file management operations by using these options such as opening, closing, saving, printing, exiting, etc. It displays the following sub menu.

Fig. 4.3

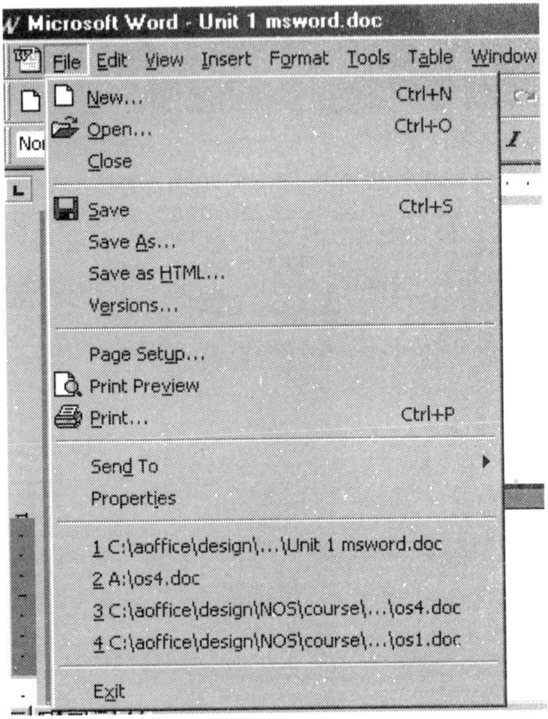

(b) Edit

Using this option you can perform editing functions such as cut, copy, paste, find and replace, etc. It displays the following sub menu.

FIG. 4.4

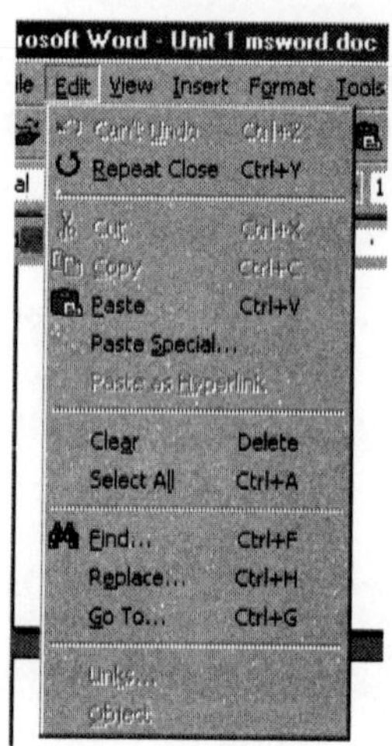

(c) View

Word document can be of many pages. The different pages may have different modes. Each mode has its

FIG. 4.5

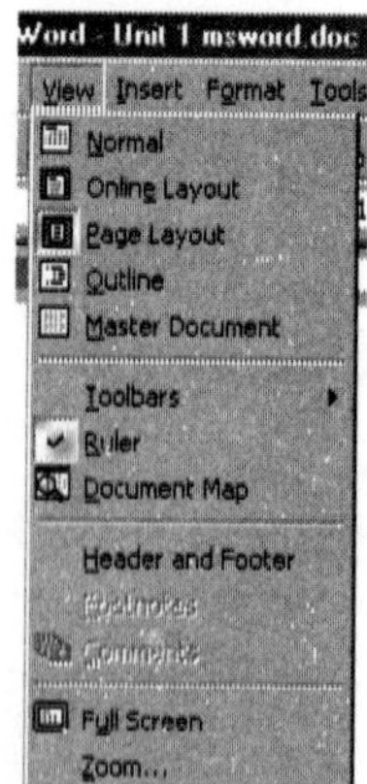

limitations. For example in normal mode the graphical picture cannot be displayed. They can only be displayed in page layout mode. Using the option "View" you can switch over from one mode to other. It displays the following Sub menu.

(d) Insert

Using this menu, you can insert various objects such as page numbers, footnotes, picture frames, etc. in your document. It displays the following Sub menu.

FIG. 4.6

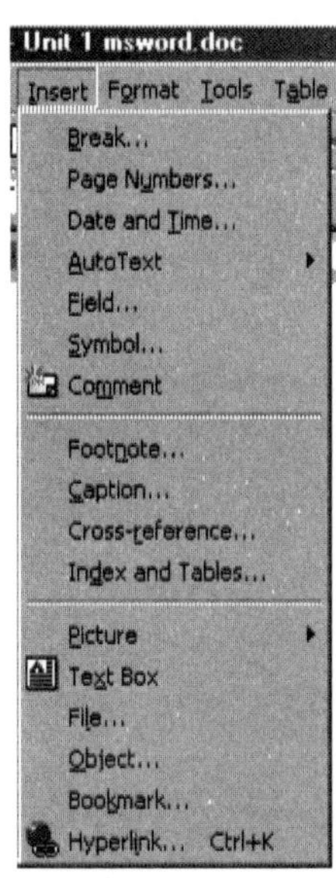

(e) Format

Using this menu, you can perform various type of formatting operations, such as fonts can be changed, borders can be framed, etc. It displays the following Sub menu. (See Figure 4.7)

(f) Tools

Using this menu, you can have access to various utilities/ tools of Word, such as spell check, macros, mail merge, etc. It displays the following Sub menu. (See Figure 4.8)

FIG. 4.7

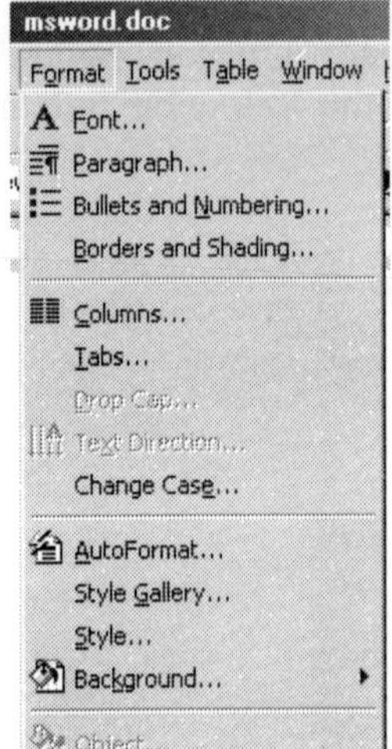

FIG. 4.8

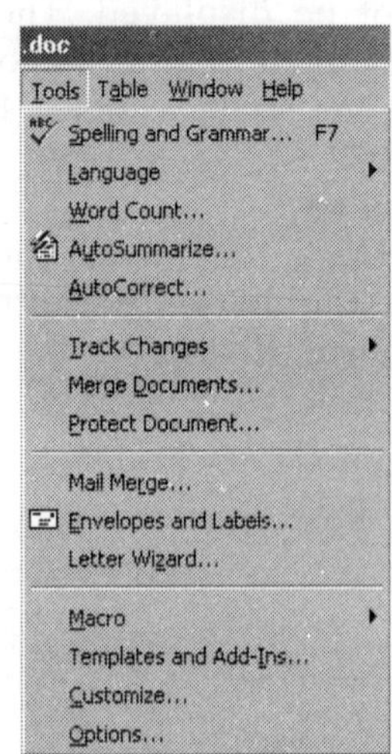

(g) Table

This menu deals with tables. Using this menu you can perform various types of operations on the table. It displays the following Sub menu.

FIG. 4.9

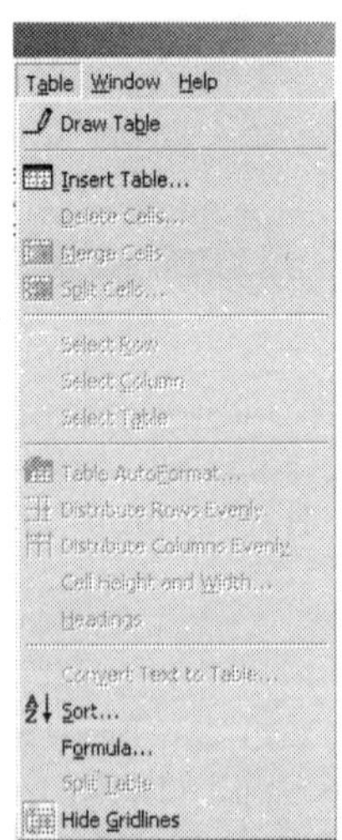

(h) Window

This menu allows you to work with two documents simultaneously. This would require two windows to be opened so that each one can hold one document. Using this menu, you can switch over from one window to another. It displays the following Sub menu.

Fig. 4.10

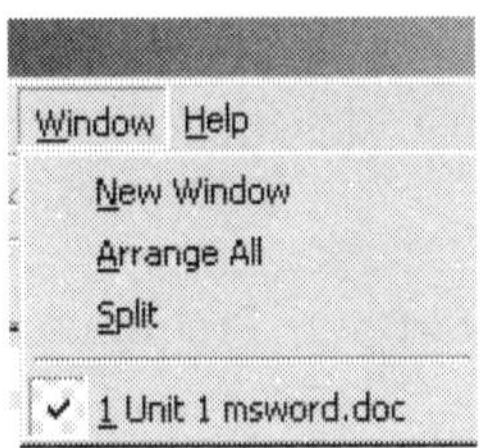

(i) Help

Using this menu, you can get on-line help for any function.

Fig. 4.11

4.7 MS EXCEL

4.7.1 Introduction into Microsoft Excel

Microsoft Excel is allows you to create professional spreadsheets and charts. It performs numerous functions and formulas to assist you in your projects.

Starting Microsoft Excel

4.7.2 Two Ways

1. Double click on the Microsoft Excel icon on the desktop.

2. Click on Start —> Programs —> Microsoft Excel

FIG. 4.12

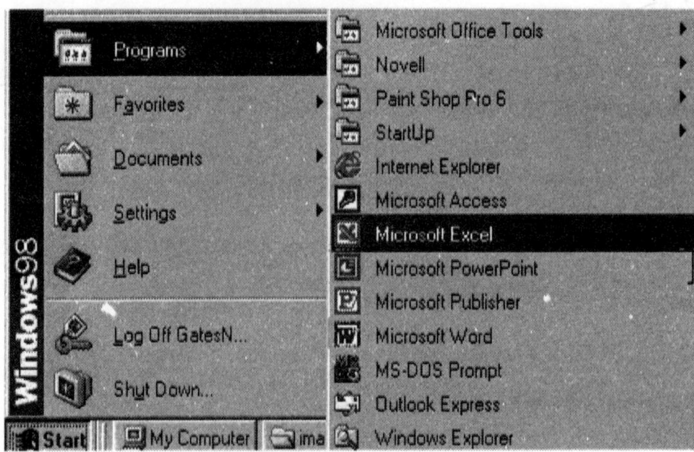

4.7.3 Creating Formulas

1. Click the cell that you want to enter the formula.
2. Type = (an equal sign).
3. Click the Function Button *fx*
4. Select the formula you want and step through the on-screen instructions.

4.7.4 Order of Operations Excel Uses

Precedence	*Operation*	*Operator*
1	Exponentiation	^
2	Multiplication	*
2	Division	/
3	Addition	+
3	Subtraction	-
4	Concatenation (putting 2 strings together, like Jenn & ifer)	&
5	Equal to	=
5	Greater Than	>
5	Less Than	<

4.7.5 Adding Borders and Shading to Cells

1. Make sure you have the **Formatting** toolbar visible
   o Click on View —> Toolbars —> Formatting
2. Select cells you wish to format by left clicking on them and highlighting them
3. Click the button to shade a cell and/or the to give a cell a border

4.8 INSERTING A CHART

1. Select over the text you want to make your chart with

FIG. 4.13

Year	State	Population
2000	Indiana	5,000,000
2000	Ohio	7,000,000
2000	Michigan	12,000,000

2. Click **Insert —> Chart.**

FIG. 4.14

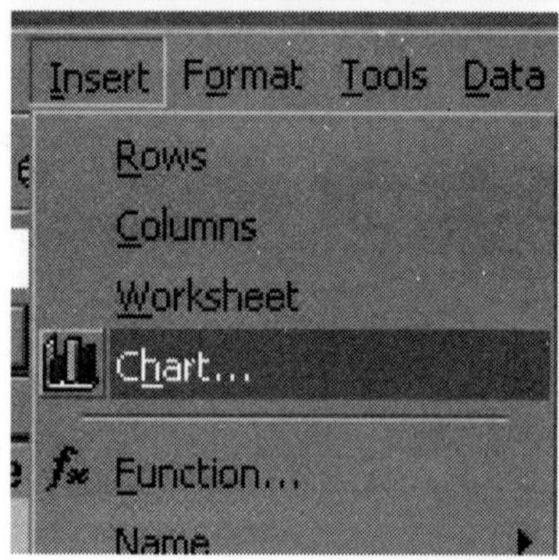

3. Select the type of chart you want.

FIG. 4.15

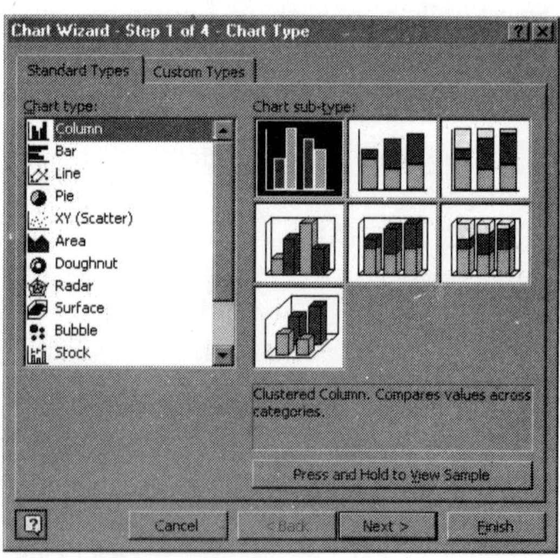

4. Confirm or change your data range Update the Chart Options.

FIG. 4.16

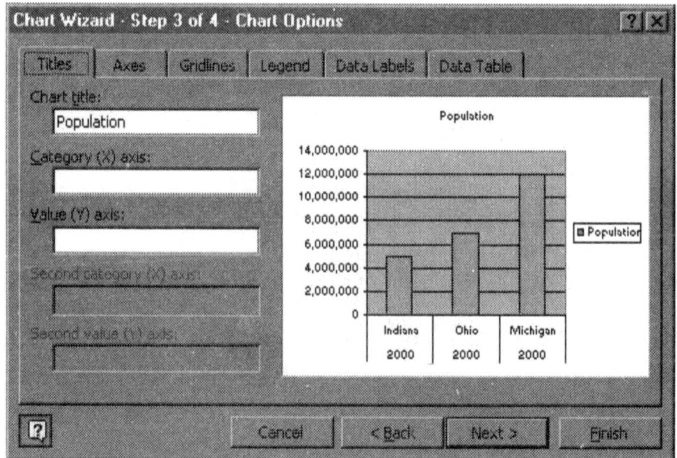

5. Select if you want to put it into the current worksheet or into a new worksheet.

FIG. 4.17

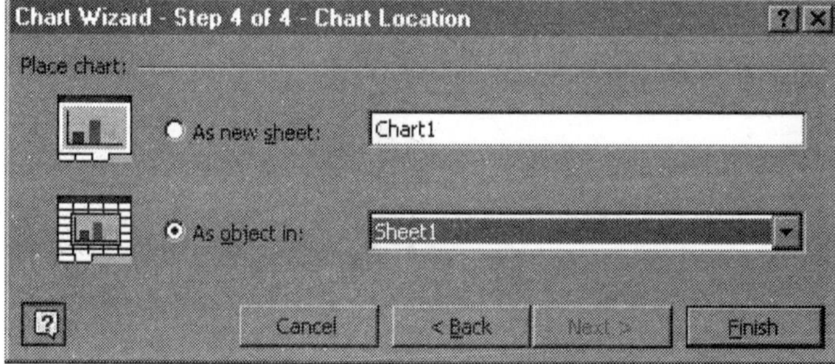

4.9 MS POWERPOINT

4.9.1 Introduction into Microsoft PowerPoint

Microsoft PowerPoint is a powerful tool to create professional looking presentations and slide shows. PowerPoint allows you to construct presentations from scratch or by using the easy to use wizard.

4.9.2 Starting Microsoft PowerPoint

Two Ways

1. Double click on the Microsoft PowerPoint icon on the desktop.

2. Click on Start —> Programs —> Microsoft PowerPoint

FIG. 4.18

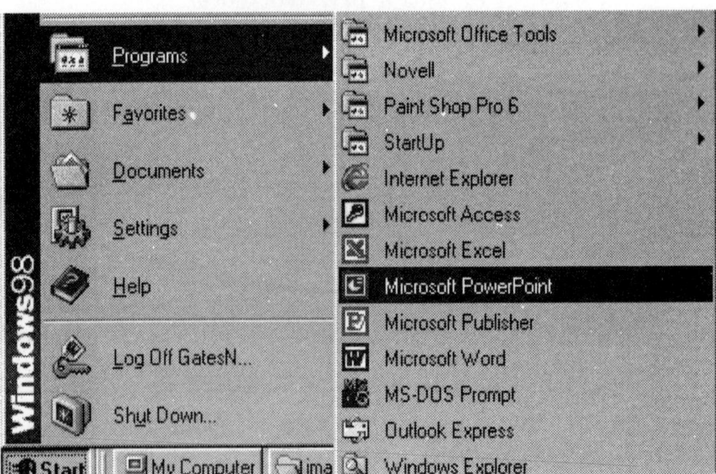

4.9.3 Creating and Opening a Presentation

After you open up Microsoft PowerPoint, a screen pops up asking if you would like to create a New Presentation or Open An Existing Presentation.

FIG. 4.19

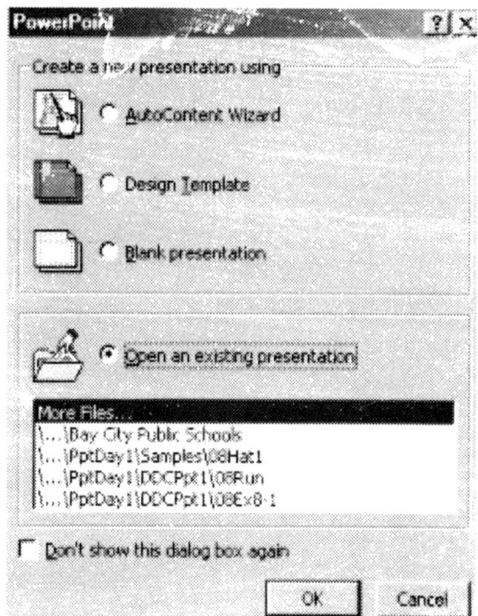

AutoContent Wizard

- Creates a new presentation by prompting you for information about content, purpose, style, handouts, and output. The new presentation contains sample text that you can replace with your own information. Simply follow the directions and prompts that are given by Microsoft PowerPoint.

Design Template

- Creates a new presentation based on one of the PowerPoint design templates supplied by Microsoft. Use what is already supplied by Microsoft PowerPoint and change the information to your own.

Blank Presentation

- Creates a new, blank presentation using the default settings for text and colors. Go to next step.

4.9.4 Opening an Existing Presentation

1. Select **Open An Existing Presentation** from the picture above.
2. Click on your presentation in the white box below step 1.
   - If you do not see your presentation in the white box, select **More Files** and hit OK.
   - Locate you existing Presentation and hit the **Open** button.

4.9.5 Create a Blank Presentation

After you select Blank Presentation a window pops up asking you to select the layout of the first slide.

FIG. 4.20

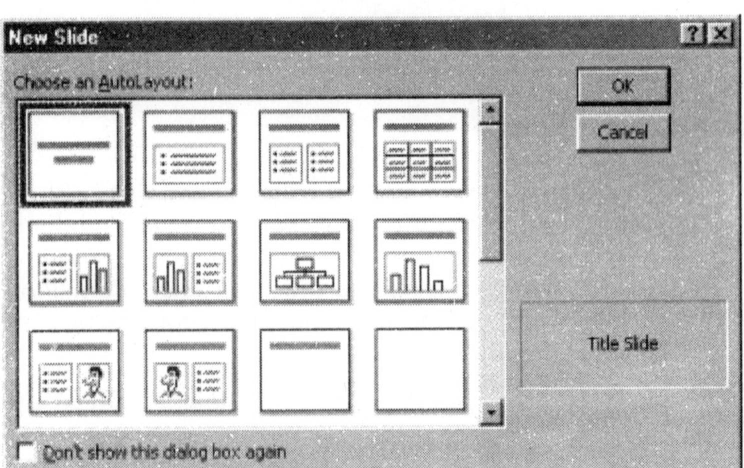

Pre-Designed Slide Layouts (Left to Right)

- Title Slide
- Bulleted List
- Two Column Text
- Table
- Text & Chart
- Chart & Text

- Organizational Chart
- Chart
- Text & Clip Art
- Clip Art & Text
- Title Only
- Blank Slide

Note : *If you already know what you want in your next slide, it is a very good idea to choose one of the pre-designed layouts from above. However if you do not, then you can still insert what you want in throughout your Presentation anytime you desire. Just choose Blank Slide and insert items as you see fit.*

4.9.6 Different Views that PowerPoint Demonstrates

There are different views within Microsoft PowerPoint that allow you to look at your presentation from different perspectives.

FIG. 4.21

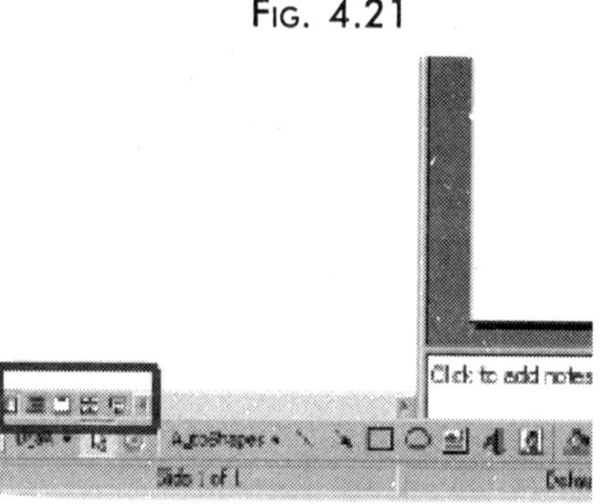

Normal View

Switches to normal view, where you can work on one slide at a time or organize the structure of all the slides in your presentation.

Outline View

Switches to outline view, where you can work with the structure of your file in outline form. Work in outline view when you need to organize the structure of your file.

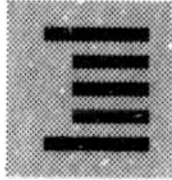

Slide View

Switches to slide view where you can work on one slide at a time.

Slide Sorter View

Displays miniature versions of all slides in a presentation, complete with text and graphics. In slide sorter view, you can recorder slides, add transitions, and animation effects. You can also set the timings for electronic slide shows.

Slide Show View

Runs you slide show in a full screen, beginning wiht the current slide if you are in slide view or the selected slide if you are in slide sorter view. If you simply want to view your show fromt he first slide.

1. Click **Slide Show** at the top of the screen.
2. Select **view show.**

Slide Manipulation

- Inserting A New Slide
  1. Click **Insert** at top of screen.
  2. Select New Slide.
- Formatting A Slide Background.
  - o You can format your slide to make it look however you would like, whether it be a background color, picture, or a design template built into Microsoft PowerPoint. The next step will show you how to apply a Design Template, but the other items mentioned above can be accomplished the same way.
    1. Click **Format** at the top of the screen
    2. Select Apply Design Template. (See Figure 4.22)
    3. Select Design you wish to apply
    4. Click Apply Button
- Inserting Clipart and Pictures

Fig. 4.22

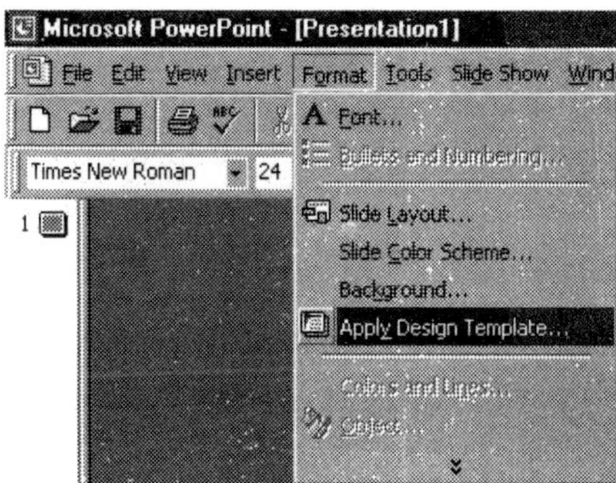

1. Display the slide you want to add a picture to
2. Click **Insert** at the top of the screen
3. Select **Picture**
4. Select **Clip Art**
5. Click the category you want
6. Click the picture you want
7. Click Insert Clip on the shortcut menu
8. When you are finished using the Clip Gallery, click the Close button on the Clip Gallery title bar
9. Steps 1-4 are very similar when inserting other Pictures, Objects, Movies, Sounds, and Charts

4.9.7 Adding Transitions to a Slide Show

You can add customized transitions to your slide show that will make it come alive and become appealing to your audience. Follow these steps when adding Slide Transitions.

1. In **slide or slide sorter view**, select the slide or slides you want to add a transition to.
2. On the **Slide Show** menu at the top of the screen, click **Slide Transition.**
3. In the Effect box, click the transition you want, and then select any other options you want.
4. To apply the transition to the selected slide, click Apply.

Fig. 4.23

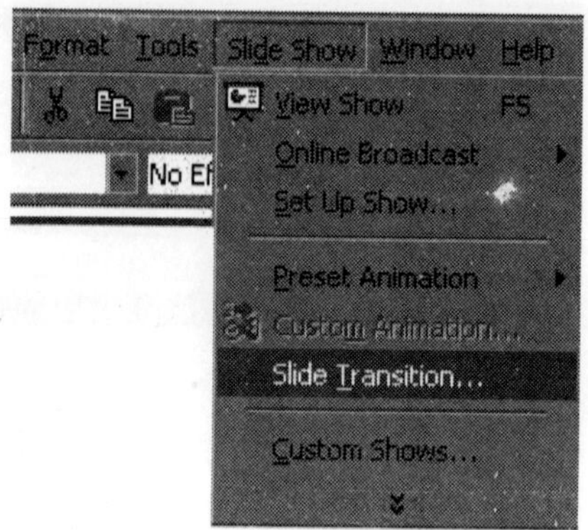

5. To apply the transition to all the slides, click Apply to All.
6. Repeat the process for each slide you want to add a transition to.
7. To view the transitions, on the Slide Show menu, click Animation Preview.

4.10 VIEWING THE SLIDE SHOW

You can view your slide show by any of the following ways:

1. Click Slide Show at the lower left of the PowerPoint window.
2. On the Slide Show menu, click View Show.
3. On the View menu, click Slide Show.
4. Press F5 on the keyboard.

4.11 NAVIGATING WHILE IN YOUR SLIDE SHOW

- **Forward Navigation**
  - o Simply click on the left Mouse Button or hit the Enter Button on your keyboard.
- **Reverse Navigation**
  - o Hit the Backspace on the keyboard.

- **Exiting the show**
  - o Hit the Esc Button on the keyboard.

4.12 PACK UP A PRESENTATION FOR USE ON ANOTHER COMPUTER

1. Open the Presentation you want to pack.
2. On the **File** menu, click **Pack and Go.**
3. Follow the instructions in the Pack and Go Wizard.

4.13 UNPACK A PRESENTATION TO RUN ON ANOTHER COMPUTER

1. Insert the disk or connect to the network location you packed the presentation to.
2. In My Computer, go to the location of the packed presentation, and then double-click **Pngsetup**.
3. Enter the destination you want to copy the presentation.

4.14 MS ACCESS

4.14.1 Microsoft Access Description

- Microsoft Access is a powerful program to create and manage your databases. It has many built in features to assist you in constructing and viewing your information. Access is much more involved and is a more genuine database application than other programs such as Microsoft Works.
  First of all you need to understand how Microsoft Access breaks down a database. Some keywords involved in this process are: *Database File, Table, Record, Field, Data-type*. Here is the Hierarchy that Microsoft Access uses in breaking down a database.

Database File : This is your main file that encompasses the entire database and that is saved to your hard-drive or floppy disk. Example) StudentDatabase.mdb.

Table : A table is a collection of data about a specific topic. There can be multiple tables in a database. Example #1) Students Example #2) Teachers.

Field : Fields are the different categories within a Table. Tables usually contain multiple fields. Example #1) Student LastName Example #2) Student FirstName.

Datatypes : Datatypes are the properties of each field. A field only has 1 datatype. FieldName) Student LastName Datatype) Text.

FIG. 4.24

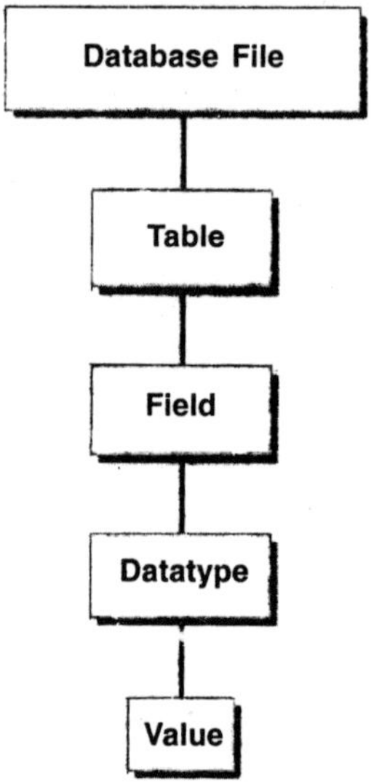

Database File

Table

Field

Datatype

Value

4.14.2 Starting Microsoft Access

- Two Ways.
  1. Double click on the Microsoft Access icon on the desktop.

2. Click on Start —> Programs —> Microsoft Access.

Fig. 4.25

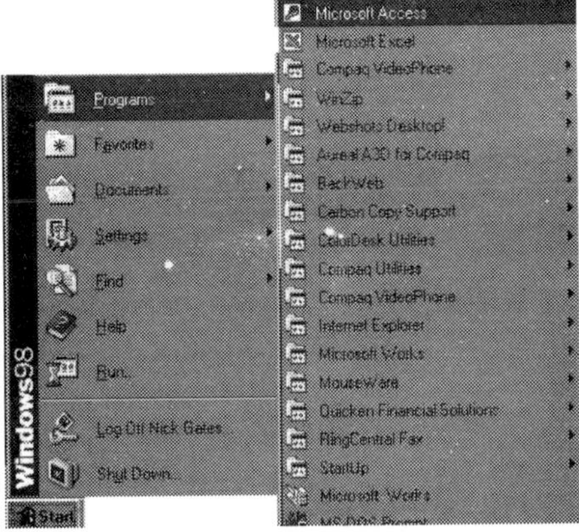

4.14.3 Creating New, and Opening Existing Databases

The above picture gives you the option to:

Fig. 4.26

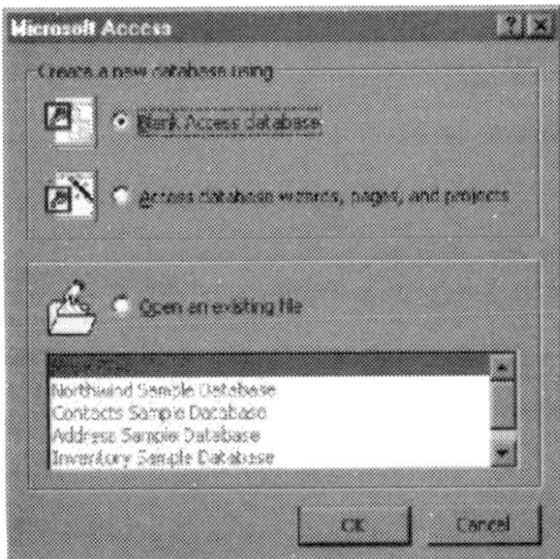

- Create a New Database from scratch
- Use the wizard to create a New Database
- Open an existing database

- The white box gives you the most recent databases you have used. If you do not see the one you had created, choose the More Files option and hit OK. Otherwise choose the database you had previously used and click OK.

4.14.4 Create a Database using the Database Wizard

1. When Microsoft Access first starts up, a dialog box is automatically displayed with options to create a new database or open an existing one. If this dialog box is displayed, click **Access Database Wizards, pages, and projects** and then click **OK.**
   If you have already opened a database or closed the dialog box that displays when Microsoft Access starts up, click **New Database** on the toolbar.
2. On the **Databases** tab, double-click the icon for the kind of database you want to create.
3. Specify a name and location for the database.
4. Click **Create** to start defining your new database

4.14.5 Create a Database without using the Database Wizard

1. When Microsoft Access first starts up, a dialog box is automatically displayed with options to create a new database or open an existing one. If this dialog box is displayed, click **Blank Access Database,** and then click **OK.** If you have already opened a database or closed the dialog box that displays when Microsoft Access starts up, click **New Database** on the toolbar, and then double-click the **Blank Database** icon on the **General** tab.
2. Specify a name and location for the database and click **Create.** (Below is the screen that shows up following this step).

FIG. 4.27

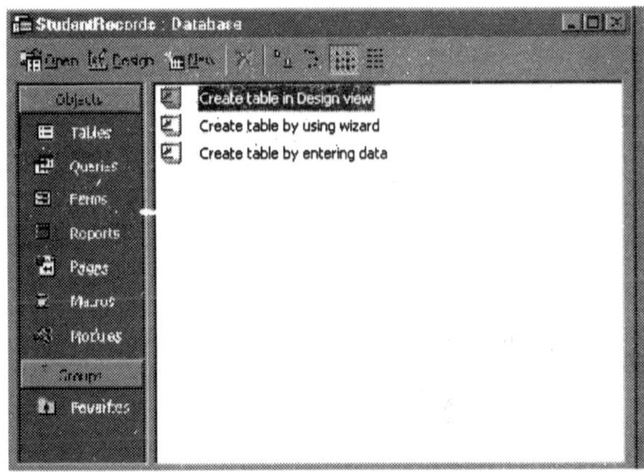

4.14.6 Tables

A table is a collection of data about a specific topic, such as students or contacts. Using a separate table for each topic means that you store that data only once, which makes your database more efficient, and reduces data-entry errors.

Tables organize data into columns (called fields) and rows (called records).

FIG. 4.28

Student Records Table

Soc Sec #	First Name	Last Name	BirthDate	Address	City
123456789	Todd	Jones	1/1/78	312 Wenona Rd	Bay City
315465866	Alan	Craig	2/8/80	123 N Union	Bay City
968585471	Stacy	Evans	3/8/81	RR 5 Box 880	Auburn
848131523	John	Anderson	4/5/80	83 Washington Dr.	Midland

4.14.7 Create a Table from Scratch in Design View

1. If you haven't already done so, switch to the Database Window You can press F11 to switch to the Database window from any other window.

FIG. 4.29

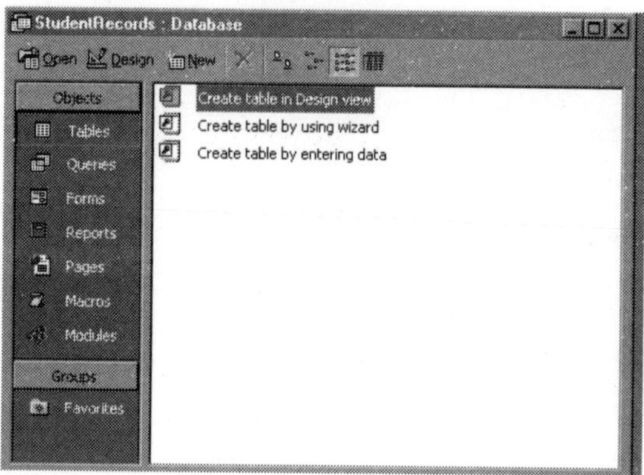

2. Double-Click on **"Create table in Design view"**. *(DESIGN VIEW)*
3. Define each of the fields in your table.
   - o Under the Field Name column, enter the categories of your table.
   - o Under Data Type column, enter the type you want for you categories.
     - ▪ The attribute of a variable or field that determines what kind of data it can hold. For example, in a Microsoft Access database, the Text and Memo field data types allow the field to store either text or numbers, but the Number data type will allow the field to store numbers only. Number data type fields store numerical data that will be used in mathematical calculations. Use the Currency data type to display or calculate currency values. Other data types are Date/Time, Yes/No, Auto Number, and OLE object (Picture).
   - o Under the Description column, enter the text that describes what you field is. (This field is optional).
   - o For our tutorial enter the following items:

Fig. 4.30

Field Name	Data Type	Description
Soc Sec #	Text	Social Security Number. Uniquely identifies a student
First Name	Text	Student's First Name
Last Name	Text	Student's Last Name
BirthDate	Date/Time	Student's Birthdate
Address	Text	Students Address
City	Text	City student resides in
State	Text	State student resides in
Zip	Text	Zip Code student resides in
Phone	Text	Student's home phone number

4.14.8 Primary Key

- One or more fields (columns) whose value or values uniquely identify each record in a table. A primary key does not allow Null values and must always have a unique value. A primary key is used to relate a table to foreign keys in other tables.
- **NOTE:** You do not have to define a primary key, but it's usually a good idea. If you don't define a primary key, Microsoft Access asks you if you would like to create one when you save the table.
- For our tutorial, make the Soc Sec # field the primary key, meaning that every student has a social security number and no 2 are the same.
  - o To do this, simply select the Soc Sec # field and select the primary key button

  - o After you do this, Save the table

Switching Views

- To switch views form the datasheet (spreadsheet view) and the design view, simply click the button in the top-left hand corner of the Access program.

Datasheet View

Displays the view, which allows you to enter raw data into your database table.

Design View

Displays the view, which allows you to enter fields, data-types, and descriptions into your database table.

Entering Data

- Click on the Datasheet View and simply start "chugging" away by entering the data into each field. **NOTE:** Before starting a new record, the **Soc Sec #** field must have something in it, because it is the Primary Key. If you did not set a Primary Key then it is OK.

Fig. 4.31

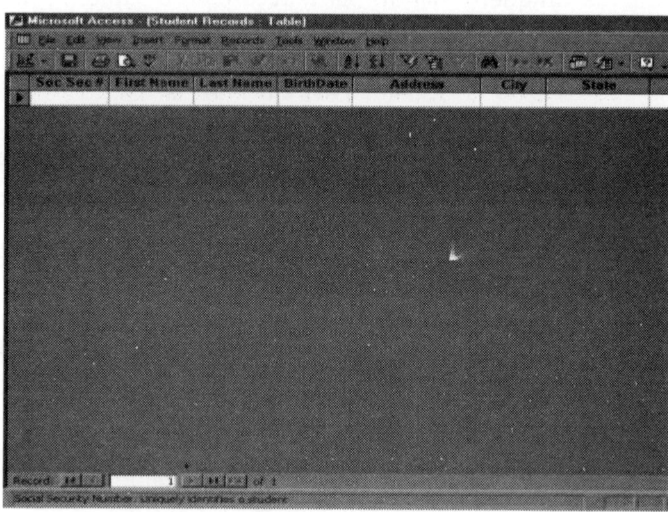

Manipulating Data

- **Adding a new row**
  - o Simply drop down to a new line and enter the information.
- **Updating a record**
  - o Simply select the record and field you want to update, and change its data with what you wan .

- **Deleting a record.**
  - o Simply select the entire row and hit the Delete Key on the keyboard.

Advanced Table Features w/Microsoft Access

- **Assigning a field a specific set of characters**
  - o Example) Making a Social Security Number only allows 9 characters.
    1. Switch to Design View.
    2. Select the field you want to alter.
    3. At the bottom select the General Tab.

Fig. 4.32

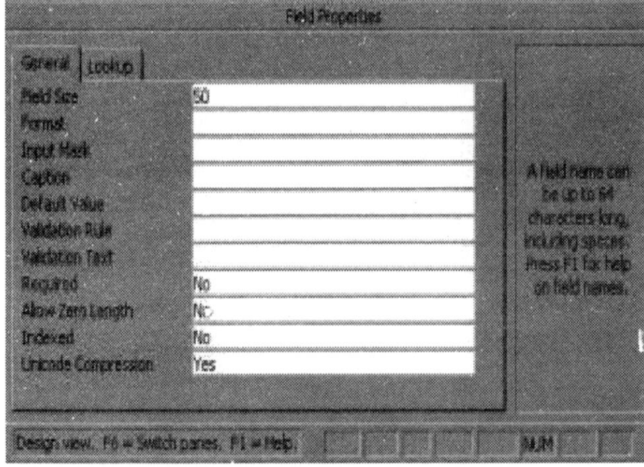

4. Select **Field Size**
5. Enter the number of characters you want this field to have

- **Formatting a field to look a specific way (HINT: You do not need to assign a field a specific set of characters if you do this)**
  - o Example) Formatting Phone Number w/Area Code (xxx) xxx-xxxx
    1. Switch to Design View

2. Select the field you want to format.
3. At the bottom select the General Tab.
4. Select **Input Mask Box** and click on the ... button at the right.
5. Select Phone Number option.

FIG. 4.33

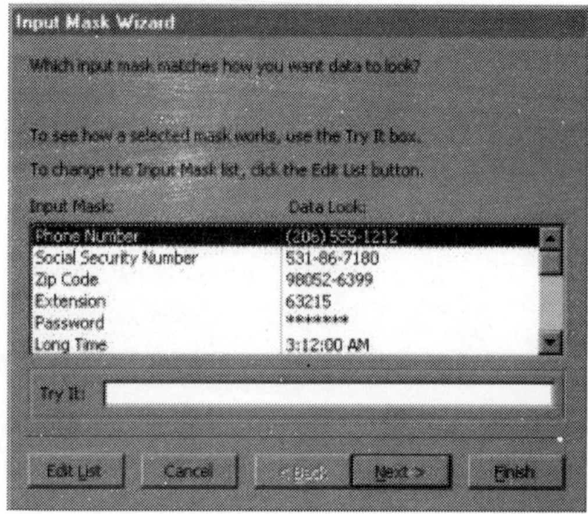

6. Click on Next.
7. Leave !(999) 000-0000 the way it is. This is a default.
8. Click Next.
9. Select which option you want it to look like.
10. Click Next.
11. Click Finish.

- **Selecting a value from a dropdown box with a set of values that you assign to it. This saves you from typing it in each time**
   - o Example) Choosing a city that is either Auburn, Bay City, Flint, Midland, or Saginaw.
     1. Switch to Design View.
     2. Select the field you want to alter (City).
     3. At the bottom select the Lookup Tab.
     4. In the **Display Control** box, select **Combo Box.**

5. Under **Row Source Type,** select **Value List.**
6. Under **Row Source,** enter the values how you want them displayed, separated by a comma. (Auburn, Bay City, Flint, Midland, Saginaw).

- ***Note :*** This will not alphabetize them for you, so you will have to do that yourself. It should look something like this:

FIG. 4.34

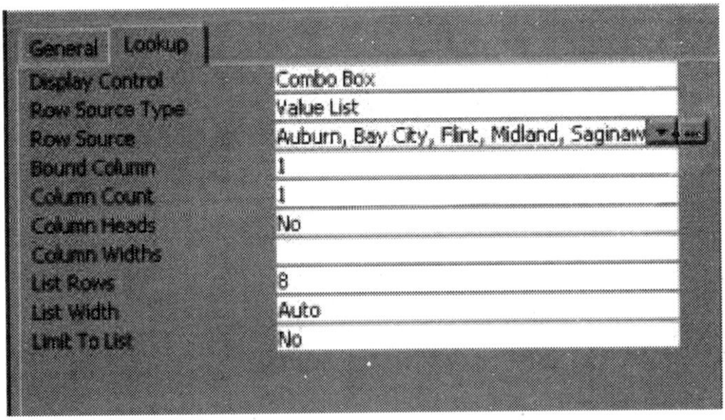

7. Select in the datasheet view and you should see the change when you go to the city field.

FIG. 4.35

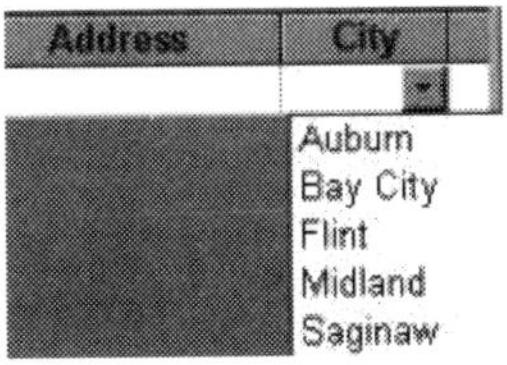

4.14.9 Relationships

After you've set-up multiple tables in your Microsoft Access database, you need a way of telling Access how to bring that information back together again. The first step in this process is to define relationships between your tables. After you've done that, you can create queries, forms, and reports to display information from several tables at once.

A relationship works by matching data in key fields—usually a field with the same name in both tables. In most cases, these matching fields are the primary key from one table, which provides a unique identifier for each record, and a foreign key in the other table. For example, teachers can be associated with the students they're responsible for by creating a relationship between the teacher's table and the student's table using the TeacherID fields.

Having met the criteria above, follow these steps for creating relationships between tables.

1. In the database window view, at the top, click on Tools —> Relationships.
2. Select the Tables you want to link together, by clicking on them and selecting the Add Button.
3. Drag the primary key of the Parent table (Teacher in this case), and drop it into the same field in the Child table (Student in this case).

FIG. 4.36

4. Select **Enforce Referential Integrity**

FIG. 4.37

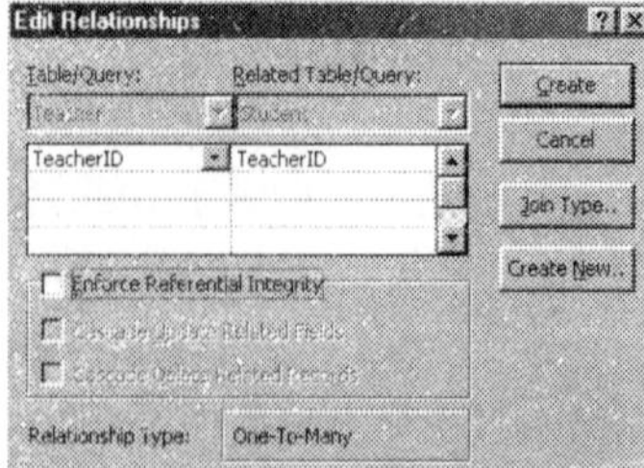

- o When the Cascade Update Related Fields check box is set, changing a primary key value in the primary table automatically updates the matching value in all related records.
- o When the Cascade Delete Related Records check box is set, deleting a record in the primary table deletes any related records in the related table.

5. Click Create and Save the Relationship.

4.14.10 Forms

A form is nothing more than a graphical representation of a table. You can add, update, delete records in your table by using a form. **NOTE:** Although a form can be named different from a table, they both still manipulate the same information and the same exact data. Hence, if you change a record in a form, it will be changed in the table also.

A form is very good to use when you have numerous fields in a table. This way you can see all the fields in one screen, whereas if you were in the table view (datasheet) you would have to keep scrolling to get the field you desire.

4.14.11 Create a Form using the Wizard

It is a very good idea to create a form using the wizard, unless you are an advanced user and know what you are doing. Microsoft Access does a very good job of creating a form using the wizard. The following steps are needed to create a basic form:

1. Switch to the Database Window. You can do this by pressing F11 on the keyboard.
2. Click on the **Forms** button under **Objects** on the left side of screen.
3. Double click on **Create Form Using Wizard.**
4. On the next screen select the fields you want to view on your form. Most of the time you would select all of them.
5. Click Next.
6. Select the layout you wish.
7. Click Next.
8. Select the style you desire...**HINT**: if you plan on

printing your form, I suggest you use a light background to save on printer toner and ink.

9. Click Next.
10. Give you form a name, and select **Open the Form and enter information.**
11. Select **Finish.**
12. You should see your form. To adjust the design of your form, simply hit the design button (same as with the tables), and adjust your form accordingly.

4.14.12 Reports

A report is an effective way to present your data in a printed format. Because you have control over the size and appearance of everything on a report, you can display the information the way you want to see it.

4.14.13 Create a Report using the Wizard

As with the Form, it is a very good idea to create a report using the wizard, unless you are an advanced user. Microsoft Access does a very good job using the wizard to create reports.

1. Switch to the Database Window. You can do this by pressing F11 on the keyboard.
2. Click on the **Reports** button under **Objects** on the left side of screen.
3. Double click on **Create Report Using Wizard.**
4. On the next screen select the fields you want to view on your form. Most of the time you would select all of them.
5. Click Next.
6. Select if you would like to group your files. Keep repeating this step for as many groupings as you would like.
7. Click Next.
8. Select the layout and the paper orientation you desire.
9. Click Next.
10. Select the style you desire...**HINT**: if you plan on printing your report, I suggest you use a light background to save on printer toner and ink.

11. Click Next.
12. Give you report a name, and select **Preview the Report.**
13. Select **Finish.**
14. You should see your report. To adjust the design of your report, simply hit the design button (same as with the tables), and adjust your report accordingly.

4.14.14 Creating Mail Merge Labels using a Wizard

Microsoft Access lets you create Mailing Labels for your database that you have. To do this do the following:

1. Switch to the Database Window. You can do this by pressing F11 on the keyboard.
2. Click on the **Reports** button under **Objects** on the left side of screen.
3. Click on **New.**

FIG. 4.38

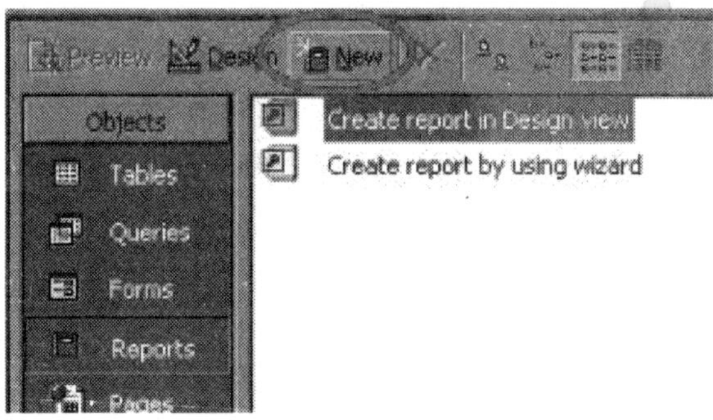

4. Select **Label Wizard** and the table you would like to get your information from. (See Figure 4.39)
5. Click OK
6. Select the layout of your labels
7. Click Next
8. Select the font size and color you want on each label
9. Click Next
10. Select how you want your label to look
11. Click Next

Fig. 4.39

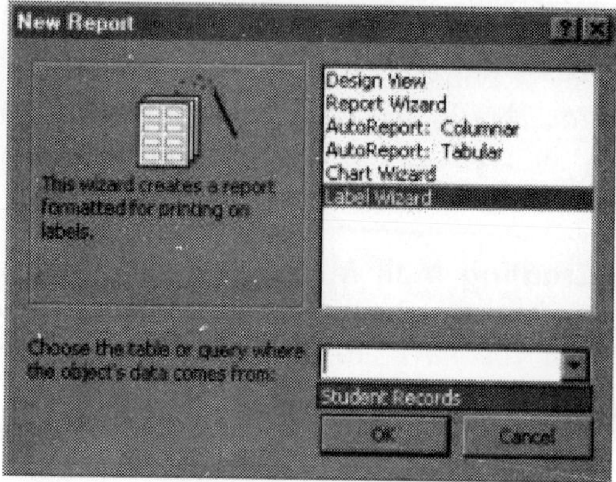

12. Select how you want your labels sorted.
13. Give your label report a name and preview it.

4.14.15 MS Publisher

Introduction into Microsoft Publisher

Microsoft Publisher 2000 helps you easily create, customize, and publish materials such as newsletters, brochures, flyers, catalogs, and Web sites. Publish easily on your desktop printer.

4.14.16 Starting Microsoft Publisher

Two Ways

1. Double click on the Microsoft Publisher icon on the desktop.

2. Click on Start —> Programs —> Microsoft Publisher.

FIG. 4.40

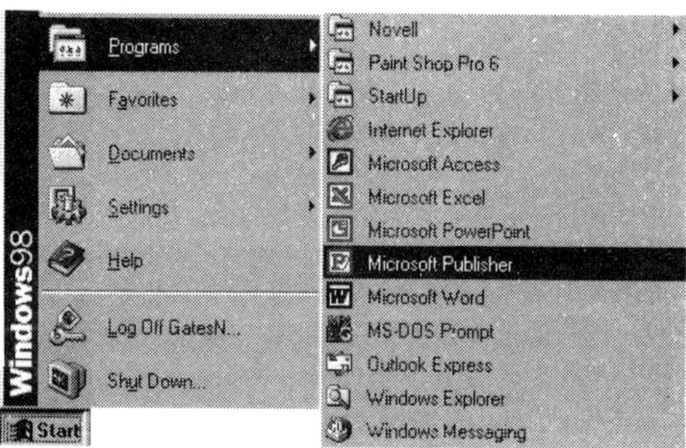

4.14.17 Creating a Publication Using a Wizard

1. On the **File** menu, click **New**.
2. Click the **Publications by Wizard** tab.

3. In the Wizards pane, click the type of publication you want.
4. In the right pane, click the design you want.
5. Click **Start Wizard**.
6. To make changes to the publication's color scheme, layout, or personal information now, click **Next** and step through the wizard's questions to make the desired changes.
7. When you finish making changes, click **Finish**.
8. In you publication replace the placeholder text and pictures with your own or with other objects.
9. On the **File** menu, click **Save**.
10. In the **Save In** box, select the folder where you want to save the new publication.
11. In the **File name** box, type a name for your publication.
12. Click Save.

4.14.18 Using the Quick Publication Wizard with a Blank Publication

1. On the **File** menu, click **New**
2. In the Catalog, click **Blank Publications**
3. Click the publication type you want and then click **Create**
4. In the **Quick Publication Wizard** pane, click the option you want
5. In the bottom pane, follow the instructions provided
6. Repeat steps 4 and 5 for each option
7. On the **File** menu, click **Save**
8. In the **Save In** box, select the folder where you want to save the new publication
9. In the **File name** box, type a name for your publication
10. Click Save

4.14.19 Create a New Publication based on a Template

1. On the **File** menu, click **New**
2. Click **Templates**
3. Double-click the template you want to use for your publication. (*Publisher opens a copy of the template*)
4. Make the changes you want to create a new publication
5. On the **File** menu, click **Save**
6. In the **Save In** box, select the folder where you want to save the new publication
7. In the **File name** box, type a name for your publication
8. Click Save

4.14.20 Start a Publication from Scratch

1. On the **File** menu, click **New**
2. Click the **Blank Publications** tab
3. Click the publication type you want and then click **Create** OR If you do not see the type of publication

you want, click **Custom Page** at the bottom of the Catalog, and then choose the options you want
4. On the **File** menu, click **Save**
5. In the **Save In** box, select the folder where you want to save the new publication
6. In the **File name** box, type a name for your publication
7. Click Save

4.14.21 Open an Existing Publication

1. On the **File** menu, click **Open**
2. Click the publications you want to open, and then click **Open**. *If you do not see the file you want, switch to the drive or folder you previously saved it in.*

4.14.22 Create a Table and Type Text into it

1. On the **Objects** toolbar, click the **Table Frame Tool**

2. Position the pointer where you want a corner of the table to appear, and then drag the mouse diagonally
3. In the **Create Table** dialog box, choose the options you want. As you click different table formats, the **Sample** box displays them
4. Click **OK**
5. In the table, click where you want to add text, and

then start typing. (The table automatically expands when your text fills the cell, unless you lock the table)

6. Move to the next cell you want to type in

4.14.23 Pack your Publication to take to Another Computer

1. On the **File** menu, point to **Pack and Go**, and then click **Take to Another Computer**. The Pack and Go Wizard takes you through each step of the packing process. Click **Next** to move to the next step. *If you haven't saved your publication already, the wizard will ask you to save it.*
2. If you're taking your publication on disk to another computer, when the wizard asks you to choose a location for saving your file, click **A: OR** If you're putting your files on an external drive, on a network, or on your computer's hard disk, click **Browse**, choose the drive and folder you want, and then click **OK.**
3. Click **Next.**
4. To embed TrueType fonts and to create links for embedded graphics, click the options you want and add a check mark. OR To not include linked graphics, click to remove the check mark.
5. Click **Next.**
6. Click **Finish.**
7. In Publisher cannot find a linked graphic while packing your publication do one of the following:
   - o Click **Retry** after you insert the disk or CD-ROM containing the original graphic into the appropriate drive.
   - o Click **Skip** to leave the current link and replace the graphic later
   - o Click **Browse** to locate a graphic that has been moved or to select another graphic and link it.
8. Insert another disk if Publisher prompts you, and click **OK**. *Remember the ordering of your disks for when you unpack them.*

9. Click **OK.**
10. **Unpack.exe** is the program you use to unpack your files, which will be on the first disk.

4.14.24 Set-up a Publication for Black and White Commercial Printing

1. On the **Tools** menu, point to **Commercial Printing Tools**, and then click **Color Printing.**
   - o **Black and White Printing.**
     1. In the **Print all colors as** box, click **Spot color(s)**, and then click **Change Spot Color.**
     2. In the **Choose Spot Color** dialog box, click **Black and white only**.
     3. Click **OK** twice.
   - o **Process-color printing.**
     1. In the **Print all colors** as box, click **Process colors (CMYK)**.
     2. Click **OK.**
   - o **Spot-color printing.**
     1. In the **Print all colors** as box, click **Spot color(s)**, and then click **Change Spot Color**.
     2. In the **Choose Spot Color** dialog box, click the arrow next to **Spot color 1**, and then choose the color you want.
     3. To choose a color that is not currently used in the publication, click **More Colors**, choose the color you want, and then click **OK.**
     4. To choose a **second spot color**, click the check box to the left of **Spot color 2**, and then click the arrow to the right and click the **second spot color.**
     5. Click **OK** twice.

5

CDS/ISIS Formating Language

5.1 INTRODUCTION

5.1.1 Versions of CDS/ISIS for Dos and Windows

CDS/ISIS for Windows is an information retrieval package developed by UNESCO (the United Nations Educational, Scientific and Cultural Organization) which runs under Microsoft Windows. Version 1.4 (release 19) was circulated on CD-ROM to distributors in March 2001 and is dated January 2001. This followed version 1.3 which appeared in January 1999 and was the first formally-released version of the package, though beta-test versions had been available to existing licence holders for some time. Version 1.0 was released in 1998 but was only a beta-test version. The version referred to in this handbook is release 19b which is available to licence holders from UNESCO's FTP site and which corrected some bugs in release 19. The package has many features which distinguish it from commercially-produced software. To understand why, it is necessary to look at the history of the package.

CDS/ISIS for Microcomputers was released by UNESCO in 1985. It was called officially CDS/ISIS Mini-Micro Version but is usually called CDS/ISIS or simply ISIS. In Latin America, where the minicomputer package MINISIS (developed in Ottawa, Canada, by the International Development Research Centre) is prevalent, the original DOS version was always called Micro-ISIS; the Windows version is called Micro-ISIS or WINISIS.

5.2 CDS/ISIS FOR DOS

The first version of the package consisted in effect of five programs which were run separately, but which acted on the same database. One program included data entry and information retrieval and the remaining corresponded to the other options on the main menu of later DOS versions, Sorting and Printing, Data Base Definition, Masterfile Services and System Utility Services. In 1988 version 2.0 was released. It was little more than an amalgamation of the different programs into one but with the addition of Pascal programming to enable additional functions to be added to the basic package. The next public release was version 2.3 which included improvements in the speed of the indexing and in the space used by the indexes. This was achieved in part by setting up two indexes, one for short and one for long terms. At the same time the package was made more resilient; hitherto a database could be irreparably corrupted if a power failure occurred while a record was being entered. The database then had to be restored from the previous back-up. This changed because from version 2.3 the files containing a database are closed after each record is modified or added.

5.3 CDS/ISIS FOR WINDOWS

Since 1989, when most new microcomputers were supplied with a new operating system called Microsoft Windows, it was inevitable that the users of CDS/ISIS would call for a Windows version, and UNESCO began to develop one in 1995. Unlike the DOS version, ISIS for Windows is not written in Pascal but in a combination of languages, primarily C and C++. Following the philosophy of the DOS version, a program library is available of programs which can be utilized in the user's own routines in a similar way to that in which Pascal was used in the DOS version.

5.4 WWWISIS

Mention of BIREME obliges us to note the existence of a version of CDS/ISIS which allows CDS/ISIS databases to be searched in client/server mode, the 'server' being a web-server and the 'client' a personal computer running any web-browser: Netscape and Microsoft Internet Explorer are the most common. Little experience is required by the user of the client to search the database but the setting up of the WWWISIS software on the server requires technical skills which will usually be found in organisations which have their own a connection to the internet and hence in-house expertise in computer systems and software. WWWISIS relies on a print formatting language which is a combination of the CDS/ISIS language and Hypertext Markup Language (HTML).

5.5 JAVAISIS

JavaISIS is another method of client/server operation which allows access to a CDS/ISIS database on any machine attached to the internet even if it not a webserver. It requires the WWWISIS server from BIREME to be on the same machine. Information on this is found at http://web.tiscalinet.it/javaisis/.

5.6 OTHER VERSIONS

UNESCO has produced versions of CDS/ISIS for VMS and UNIX operating systems. VMS is now obsolete, but the UNIX version is well used. We are not here covering any other version than the Windows version.

5.6.0 General Overview of CDS/ISIS for Windows

CDS/ISIS for Windows is, as its name implies, a Windows-based system. Windows programs have many distinctive features as a result of the Windows operating system. Microsoft Windows is described as a graphical user environment which gives you more control over the way you work as well as enabling you to use more of the power of the computer. It allows you, for example, to run more than one program at the same time. Thus it allows you to have more than one CDS/ISIS database open. Your work appears in a window which may be enlarged, diminished, activated or put on hold whilst other windows are opened and programs there run. Because more than one program may be available on the screen it is possible to transfer data or images from one to another. As well as using the computer's keyboard, the user can employ a mouse to move windows around the screen and to activate or de-activate windows. Within a Window there are drop down menus also activated by the mouse. A number of drop-down menus are accessible from the bar at the top of each window. They are accessed by a single click of the mouse with the pointer controlled by the mouse on the relevant word at the top of the window. Alternatively pressing the {Alt} key and keying the underlined letter in that word will 'open' the menu.

5.6.1 The Windows Version : The Main Menu

At this point we are assuming that CDS/ISIS for Windows has been loaded on your computer and that the machine has been switched on and Windows is running. Open the CDS/ISIS for Windows program by clicking on the WINISIS icon. This will run the program and display the main menu. Let us look at the drop-down menus from left to right. Database leads to the functions associated with a database. In other Windows programs, this would usually be F for File. If you have just opened the program by clicking on the WINISIS icon, you will have only four options, Open, New, Printer Setup and Exit. Other options are greyed out as shown in Figure 1.2. You will see them in a light shade of grey in contrast with the black of other menus. This is a convention used by most programs which run under Windows which indicates that that option is not at that time available. There may also be a list of the last five databases open on which you may also click to retrieve one. These will always be in black.

You open a database by choosing **Open**, or the icon on the very left of the tool bar, a picture of an open card file. This

FIG. 5.1

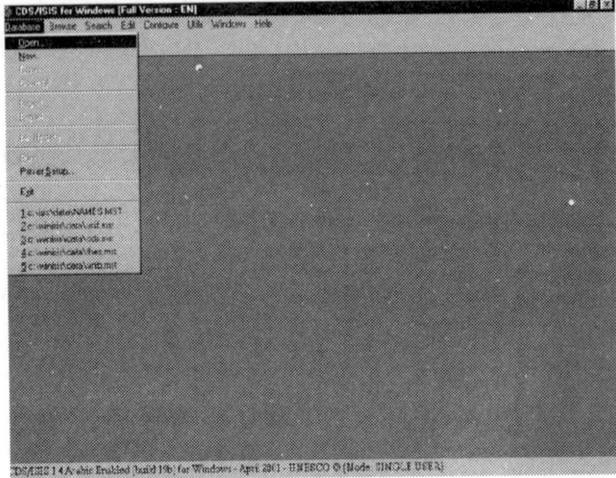

brings up a Window entitled File Selection. This is in the usual Windows format giving the possibility of browsing through drives and folders to find the appropriate 'file name' which will be an **mst** file or a **par** file. It will be set to the folder named in parameter 4 of the **syspar.par**: this is described in section 3.2. When you have clicked on a database to open it, all options under **Database** will become accessible as in Figure. You will see at the same time as a database is opened that more icons appear on the tool bar.

FIG. 5.2

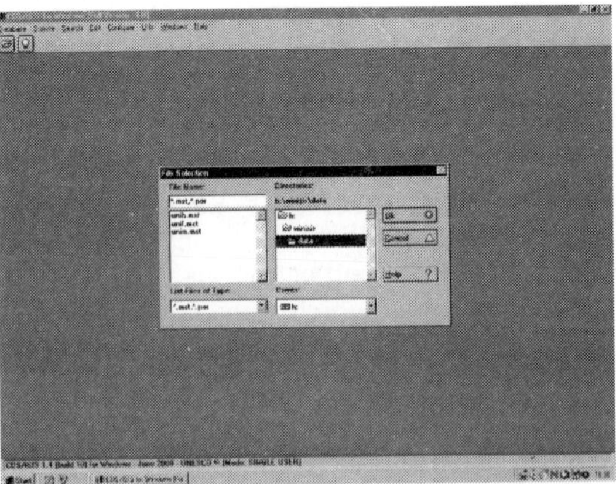

Close and **Close All** are self explanatory and result in the closing of one or all databases. The other functions which become available are **Import**, **Export**, **I/F Update** (i.e. Inverted File Update) and **Print**. Print is conventionally found on the left hand drop down menu in Windows applications and the other options here are for file maintenance, adding to a file, extracting a file and indexing the database. **Exit** will close the CDS/ISIS for Windows program and take you back to the Windows desktop.

Browse ({Alt b} from the menu bar) has nine functions which cannot be operated unless a database has been opened. Click on **Database** to view the records in a database in database order. Click on **Search results...** to go to a list of previous searches from where you may view the records retrieved by any earlier search in that session. You may mark any records that you view. Then you can click on **Marked records** to view only those that have been marked. Or you can revert to all records retrieved by selecting **All records.** You may open the dictionary by clicking on **Open dictionary** to see which terms have been indexed in which fields. **Split/Unsplit view** allows you to toggle with the lower portion showing

FIG. 5.3

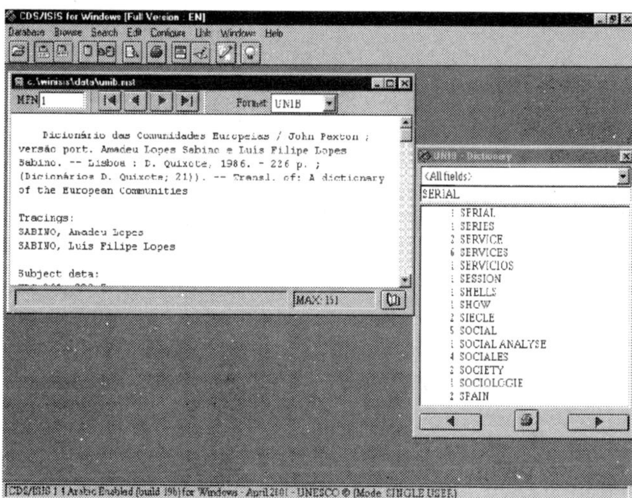

either the display in ASCII characters only or the print format specification. **Print current page** will print the record you are viewing though may not always print it quite how you see it on the screen. **Zoom In** and **Zoom out** will make the font larger or smaller. Along with **Search**, this menu is equivalent to Information Retrieval Services in CDS/ISIS for DOS. Choose **Search** {Alt s} and you will have access to two kinds of search, **Expert Search** or **Guided Search**. It also allows you to go back to a previously saved search (the search may have been saved at any previous occasion) **Recall saved search** or to save the results of the present search for future use: **Save search**. **Close Search Window** is no mystery: it allows you to close the expert or guided search window when you wish to look through the records you have retrieved.

Edit {Alt e} is the gateway to Data entry and modifying the database structure. (If you are running in *read only* mode, you will not have access to this menu.) Data entry functions are accessed by **Data entry** to call up the Data Entry window which lets you edit the record you were looking at in the browse or search window or lets you create a new record. **Delete** will delete the record you are looking at in the data entry window. You can also copy the record you have on screen into the Windows clipboard with **Copy to clipboard** or clear the clipboard by choosing **Clear clipboard**.

From this drop down menu, you can modify the database you are in via the Field Definition Table or Field Selection Tables. You can also edit or add new Print Formats.

Configure {Alt c} allows you to change the language of the menus and other features of the database including removing the ability to edit a database from the menus, to make the database read-only for that user. (The ability to read and write to the database will return next time the software is run.) You can also change many other system settings. **Utilities** {Alt u} includes global additions and deletions based on record number or a previous search. Also included is the facility to compile ISIS/Pascal programs (in CDS/ISIS for Windows these are all print format programs). You can also export records to an XML file and unlock databases or records. These unlocking functions will be greyed out and inaccessible if **Data entry** is open. **Windows** {Alt w} allows the windows open to be arranged on the screen. This is the usual Windows program facility. The windows on the screen may be arranged from left to right (horizontally) one above the other (vertically) or cascaded (one above the other but diagonally offset so that all may be seen in part and the top one in full).

Finally there is a **Help** drop down menu in the usual Windows style with a contents list and a keyword search. At the time of writing, the Help text is considerably lagging behind the current version.

5.3 AVAILABILITY OF CDS/ISIS

CDS/ISIS is protected by copyright and is in no way shareware or public domain. It can be used legally only by licence holders. This licence is not as restrictive as some commercially produced software packages, in that multiple copying of the software is permitted within an institution that is a licence holder. Nevertheless, the software should not be copied to persons or institutions which are not licence holders. When once a licence is obtained, it is valid for all versions, so new versions may legally be obtained from any source.

5.3.1 Software Contributed by Users

We have already mentioned the Pascal programming feature which is extremely important to the development and use of the DOS version of CDS/ISIS. Both DOS and Windows versions of the package include a Pascal compiler; in the case of the Windows version it can be used only for format exits.

Programs written by CDS/ISIS users to be used in conjunction with the DOS version have been made generally available. Some are offered for sale. Others are printed in journals or circulated at user group meetings. The result is that many sophisticated library automation packages have been designed, built on the basic framework of CDS/ISIS for DOS. Packages are now being developed based on CDS/ISIS for Windows and ISIS_DLL.

5.3.2 Exchange Formats

The term 'format' occurs so frequently throughout this *Handbook* that we have decided to explain it in this introduction. The term 'format' is used in many different ways in computing in general. In data processing, particularly in information retrieval packages like CDS/ISIS, it has two specialized uses. A format is an arrangement of data, and in CDS/ISIS it refers *both* to an international exchange format, especially one that is a standard format for the exchange of data between systems *and* to the layout of data as seen by the user on the screen or in printed form, called a print format or display format. Both these kinds of format are, in the bibliographic data processing field, governed by standards.

6

Search Language

6.0 INTRODUCTION

The search language offers almost all of the search functions available with **Edit > Search** described in Selecting Using the Search... Command. Searching using this command generates a search query (expressed in the search language) displayed in the **Generated query** box of the **Search** dialog box.

The search language can be used both in the power input box and in the **Advanced** tab of the **Search** dialog box but also in macros. The search query both searches for the elements and automatically selects them.

Any generated query can be run via the power input box or in macros, whether *transformat* or not.

However, the transformat query is the only usable query whatever the session language, therefore, any query you expect to run in different session languages must be written in this format.

If you are not familiar with this format, you can display its content and identify the syntax to be used prior to writing your transformat query using a hidden column (you need to drag the column separator next to the Query column to display it) in the **Favorites** tab of the **Search** dialog box:

FIG. 6.1

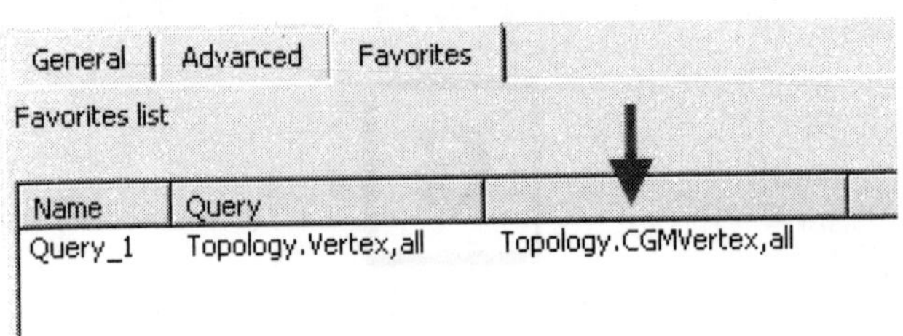

For instance, CATDrwSearch.DrwText.Name=test,in means that you will search for objects named "test" in the Drafting workbench using the "In <UI-Active object>" scope.

Search deals with the following sections:

Search Language: Syntax
Using Operating Signs
Searching by Name
Searching by Name in Graph
Searching by Type
Searching by Color
Searching by Product Properties
Searching for Objects Belonging to a Selection Set
Searching for Objects Belonging to a Layer
Searching for Visible or Hidden Elements
Searching for Line Thickness or Linetype
Searching by Symbol
Searching Using Favorites
Searching Using Predefined Favorites
Using Special Characters
Using Operators
Priority
Using Search Scopes
Using a Default Prefix
Using a Default Search Scope

6.1 SEARCH LANGUAGE: SYNTAX

You can search for objects using the same criteria as with **Edit > Search**.

The message catalog Keyboard Input. CATNls sets up the power input search syntax, and search language shortcuts. The localized version of this message catalog determines the exact syntax and shortcuts for each language.

6.2 USING OPERATING SIGNS

The search language uses the following separators (whose role you will discover in the examples below):

: and = (these separators are interchangeable)
!= (different)
<, <=, >, =>

6.3 SEARCHING BY NAME

You can search for an object name. This is particularly useful if you renamed objects using **Edit > Properties**, or the **Properties** contextual command. The name can also contain special characters.

To search for an object by its name, enter the following command:

name:*object_name* or name=*object_name*

or a command using an abbreviation referred to as a "shortcut" as follows:

n:*object_name*

where "object_name" is the name of the object.

You can also use the "*" character as a wildcard to replace any number of characters. For example, the command:

name:wheel*

searches for all objects starting with the string "wheel".

6.4 SEARCHING BY NAME IN GRAPH

You can search for an object name. This search is different from searching by name since it deals with the name as it is displayed in the specification tree.

To search for an object by its name as displayed in the specification tree, enter the following command:

name in graph=*object_name*

If you want the search to be case sensitive, enter the following command:

NAME IN GRAPH=*object_name*

6.5 SEARCHING BY TYPE

The **Type** box in the **Search** dialog box to display a list of types (the types are translated in each language).

To search for an object by its type, enter the following command:

type:*type* or type=*type*

or:

t:*type*

You can also search for types using the "." (period) as follows:

For example, entering the command:

Part Design.Pad

6.6 SEARCHING BY COLOR

You assign colors to objects using the **Color** list in the **Graphic** tab, when using **Edit > Properties** or the **Properties** contextual command. For a reminder about how to use this list, refer to Displaying and Editing Graphic Properties.

To search for an object of a specific color, enter the following command:

color:*color_name*
or:
col:*color_name*
where "color_name" is the color of the object.

6.7 SEARCHING BY PRODUCT PROPERTIES

You assign properties to products (and parts in products) by right-clicking an element in the specification tree and selecting **Properties**, clicking the **Product** tab in the **Properties** dialog box, and setting the properties in the Product frame.

The properties you can search for (the same as those you assigned to the element) are:

Part Number
Revision
Definition
Nomenclature
Product Description
Component Description.

6.8 SEARCHING FOR OBJECTS BELONGING TO A LAYER

To search for an object belonging to a specific layer (as seen in the **Graphic Properties** toolbar), enter the following command:

l:*layer_number* or l=*layer_number*
or
layer:*layer_number* or layer=*layer_number*
where "layer_number" is the number of the layer.

6.9 SEARCHING FOR OBJECTS BELONGING TO A SELECTION SET

To search for an object belonging to a selection set, enter the following command:
s:*selection_set_name*

or
set:*selection_set_name*
where "selection_set_name" is the name of the selection set.

6.10 SEARCHING FOR VISIBLE OR HIDDEN ELEMENTS

You can search for visible, invisible, shown elements, or elements hidden in the No Show space using the following syntax:

visibility:visible
vis:visible
and:
visibility:hidden
vis:hidden

6.11 SEARCHING FOR LINE THICKNESS OR LINETYPE

You can also search for objects with a specific line thickness or linetype (as seen in the **Graphic Properties** toolbar) like this:

weight:
w:
or:
dashed:
d:

When searching for lines with a specific weight, you can specify the weight index like this:

weight:6,all

6.12 SEARCHING BY SYMBOL

To search for a point symbol, enter the following command:

symbol:small full square or symbol=small full square
or
symb:small full square or symb=small full square
searches for the following point symbol:
Capital letters are meaningless for the symbol name and you can also type:
symbol:Small Full Square or symbol=SMALL FULL SQUARE

The Point Symbols you can Search for are:

Cross
Plus
Circle
Double Circle
Dot
Full Square
Star
Small Full
Square
Small Dot

6.13 SEARCHING USING FAVORITES

You can search for objects using your favorite queries defined via the Favorites tab in the **Search** dialog box. To do so:

favorite=*favorite_query_name* or
favorite:*favorite_query_name*
but you can also enter:
f=*favorite_query_name* or f:*favorite_query_name*
where "favorite_query_name" is the name of the favorite query. Note that the language used in favorite queries is case sensitive.

6.14 SEARCHING USING PRE-DEFINED FAVORITES

Before you start, note that these pre-defined favorite

queries (which deal with V5 objects only) can be neither modified, nor deleted contrary to standard favorite queries you define in the **Favorites** tab of the **Search** dialog box.

6.15 USING SPECIAL CHARACTERS

Characters & + - ( ) play a special role in the search syntax:

> To be interpreted literally in names, those characters or text strings containing those characters must be surrounded by the character '(apostrophe by default).

6.16 USING OPERATORS

The supported operators are: &, +, and – (for AND, OR and EXCEPT respectively) & ( ).

Blanks are not considered as separators. They may be surrounded by ', but this is not mandatory.

6.17 PRIORITY

There is no priority among operators, but there is a priority in their order of appearance (from left to right).

For example, the query:

> type:Part* & name:toto + type:Hole & Color:Black
> is interpreted as:
> type:Part* & (name:toto + (type:Hole & Color:Black))

6.18 USING SEARCH SCOPES

You can use the same search scopes as with **Edit > Search** (except From search results which is only available in the **Search** dialog box), by using the context aliases all, in, from, sel and scr:

> all: searches the whole specification tree from top to bottom, to find objects created using all workbenches.

in: locates the appropriate elements in the active object and in the workbench you are currently using

from: searches the elements in the active object to the bottom of the tree. For example, in a Part document, both parts and sketches are searched.

sel: if you already selected objects before selecting **Edit > Search**, this option searches from the selected objects to the bottom of the tree.

scr: searches for objects visible in the current window. Elements that are not activated or not represented in the geometry area are not taken into account.

Elements that are not represented in the geometry area are, for instance, elements transferred to the No Show space, elements that are not in the current filter or not in the current mask, features used to build other features that appear in the specification tree but not in the geometry area, etc.

6.19 USING A DEFAULT PREFIX

A prefix is required to run a command or a query via the power input box. One prefix (c:) is already provided to run commands and several prefixes are dedicated to search queries.

When searching for a name for instance, the value you type must be prefixed by n: or with name

6.20 USING A DEFAULT SEARCH SCOPE

As explained above in Using Search Scopes, the default scope is in when running a query in the power input box. This means that if no scope alias is entered at the end of the search string, the search locates the appropriate elements in the active object and in the workbench you are currently using.

7

Export and Import of Data

7.0 INTRODUCTION

Reading data into a statistical system for analysis and exporting the results to some other system for report writing can be frustrating tasks that can take far more time than the statistical analysis itself, even though most readers will find the latter far more appealing.

7.1 IMPORTS

The easiest form of data to import into package is a simple text file, and this will often be acceptable for problems of small or medium scale. The primary function to import from a text file is scan, and this underlies most of the more convenient functions discussed below. However, all statistical consultants are familiar with being presented by a client with a floppy disc or CD-R of data in some proprietary binary format, for example, 'an Excel spreadsheet' or 'an SPSS file'. Often the simplest thing to do is to use the originating application to export the data as a text file (and statistical consultants will have copies of the most common applications on their computers for that purpose).

In a few cases, data have been stored in a binary form for compactness and speed of access. One application of this that we have seen several times is imaging data, which is normally stored as a stream of bytes as represented in memory, possibly preceded by a header. Such data formats are discussed in Binary files and Binary connections. For much larger databases it is common to handle the data using a database management system (DBMS). There is once again the option of using the DBMS to extract a plain file, but for many such DBMSs the extraction operation can be done directly from an R package.

7.1.1 Export to Text Files

Exporting results from package is usually a less contentious task, but there are still a number of pitfalls. There will be a target application in mind, and normally a text file will be the most convenient interchange vehicle. Function cat underlies the functions for exporting data. It takes a file argument, and the append argument allows a text file to be written via successive calls to cat. Better, especially if this is to be done many times, is to open a file connection for writing or appending, and cat to that connection, then close it.

The most common task is to write a matrix or data frame to file as a rectangular grid of numbers, possibly with row and column labels. This can be done by the functions write. Function write just writes out a matrix or vector in a specified number of columns (and transposes a matrix). Function write is more convenient, and writes out a data frame (or an object that can be coerced to a data frame) with row and column labels. There are a number of issues that need to be considered in writing out a data frame to a text file.

1. Precision
2. Header line
3. Separator
4. Missing values
5. Quoting strings

7.2 SPREADSHEET-LIKE DATA

We saw a number of variations on the format of a spreadsheet-like text file, in which the data are presented in a rectangular grid, possibly with row and column labels. In this section we consider importing such files into R.

7.2.1 Variations on read.table

The function read.table is the most convenient way to read in a rectangular grid of data. Because of the many possibilities, there are several other functions that call read but change a group of default arguments. Beware that read is an inefficient way to read in very large numerical matrices.

Some of the issues to consider are:

1. Encoding
2. Header line
3. Separator
4. Quoting
5. Missing values
6. Unfilled lines
7. White space in character fields
8. Blank lines
9. Classes for the variables
10. Comments
11. Escapes

7.2.2 Fixed-width-format Files

Sometimes data files have no field delimiters but have fields in pre-specified columns. This very common in the days of punched cards, and is still sometimes used to save file space. Fortran is a similar function for fixed-format files, using Fortran-style column specifications.

7.2.3 Data Interchange Format (DIF)

An old format sometimes used for spreadsheet-like data is DIF, or Data Interchange format. DIF provides a simple way to read such files. It takes arguments similar to read.table for assigning types to each of the columns. In Windows, spreadsheets often store spreadsheet data on the clipboard in this format; read.DIF("clipboard") can read it from there directly. It is slightly more robust than read.table ("clipboard") in handling spreadsheets with empty cells.

7.2.4 Using Scan Directly

Both read.table and read.fwf use scan to read the file, and then process the results of scan.

They are very convenient, but sometimes it is better to use scan directly. Function scan has many arguments, most of which we have already covered under read.table. The most crucial argument is what, which specifies a list of modes of variables to be read from the file. If the list is named, the names are used for the components of the returned list.

7.2.5 Re-shaping Data

Sometimes spreadsheet data is in a compact format that gives the covariates for each subject followed by all the observations on that subject. Package modelling functions need observations in a single column.

7.2.6 Flat Contingency Tables

Displaying higher-dimensional contingency tables in array form typically is rather inconvenient. In categorical data analysis, such information is often represented in the form of bordered two-dimensional arrays with leading rows and columns specifying the combination of factor levels corresponding to the cell counts. These rows and columns are typically "ragged" in the sense that labels are only displayed when they change, with the obvious convention that rows are read from top to bottom and columns are read from left to right. In package, such "flat" contingency tables can be created using ftable, which creates objects of class "ftable" with an appropriate print method.

7.3 RELATIONAL DATABASES

7.3.1 Why use a Database?

There are limitations on the types of data that package handles well. Since all data being manipulated by package are resident in memory, and several copies of the data can be created during execution of a function, package is not well suited to extremely large data sets. Data objects that are more than a (few) hundred megabytes in size can cause package to run out of memory.

Package does not easily support concurrent access to data. That is, if more than one user is accessing, and perhaps updating, the same data, the changes made by one user will not be visible to the others. Package does support persistence of data, in that you can save a data object or an entire worksheet from one session and restore it at the subsequent session, but the format of the stored data is specific to package and not easily manipulated by other systems. Database management systems (DBMSs) and, in particular, relational DBMSs (RDBMSs) are designed to do all of these things well. Their strengths are:

1. To provide fast access to selected parts of large databases.
2. Powerful ways to summarize and cross-tabulate columns in databases.
3. Store data in more organized ways than the rectangular grid model of spreadsheets and data frames.
4. Concurrent access from multiple clients running on multiple hosts while enforcing security constraints on access to the data.
5. Ability to act as a server to a wide range of clients.

The sort of statistical applications for which DBMS might be used are to extract a 10% sample of the data, to cross-tabulate data to produce a multi-dimensional contingency table, and to extract data group by group from a database for separate analysis.

7.3.2 Overview of RDBMSs

Traditionally there have been large (and expensive) commercial RDBMSs (Informix; Oracle; Sybase; IBM's DB/2; Microsoft SQL Server on Windows) and academic and small-system databases (such as MySQL, PostgreSQL, Microsoft Access, . . .), the former marked out by much greater emphasis on data security features. The line is blurring, with the Open Source PostgreSQL having more and more high-end features, and 'free' versions of Informix, Oracle and Sybase being made available on Linux.

7.3.3 SQL Queries

The more comprehensive R interfaces generate SQL behind the scenes for common operations, but direct use of SQL is needed for complex operations in all. A relational DBMS stores data as a database of tables (or relations) which are rather similar to package data frames, in that they are made up of columns or fields of one type (numeric, character, date, currency, . . .) and rows or records containing the observations for one entity.

7.3.4 Binary Connections

Functions readBin and writeBin read to and write from binary connections. A connection is opened in binary mode by appending "b" to the mode specification, that is using mode "rb" for reading, and mode "wb" or "ab" (where appropriate) for writing.

7.3.5 Reading Excel Spreadsheets

The most common R data import/export question seems to be 'how do I read an Excel spreadsheet'. Note that most of the advice is for pre-Excel 2007 spreadsheets: currently the only one of these methods that reads the '.xlsx' format is that via RODBC.

The first piece of advice is to avoid doing so if possible! If you have access to Excel, export the data you want from Excel in tab-delimited or comma-separated form, and use read.delim or read.csv to import it into package. (You may need to use read.delim2 or read.csv2 in a continental European locale that uses comma as the decimal point.) Exporting a DIF file and reading it using read.DIF is another possibility. If you do not have Excel, many other programs are able to read such spreadsheets and export in a text format on both Windows and Unix.

You can also cut-and-paste between the display of a spreadsheet in such a program, read.table will read from the R console or, under Windows, from the clipboard (via file = "clipboard" or readClipboard). The read.DIF function can also read from the clipboard. Note that an Excel '.xls' is not just a spreadsheet: such files can contain many sheets, and the sheets can contain formulae, macros and so on. Not all readers can read other than the first sheet, and may be confused by other contents of the file. Windows users can use odbcConnectExcel in package RODBC. This can select rows and columns from any of the sheets in an Excel spreadsheet file.

Digital Library

8.0 INTRODUCTION

The term 'Digital Library' is currently used to refer to systems that are heterogeneous in scope and yield very different functionality. These systems range from digital object and metadata repositories, reference-linking systems, archives, and content administration systems (mainly developed by industry) to complex systems that integrate advanced digital library services (mainly developed in research environments). This 'overloading' of the term 'Digital Library' is a consequence of the fact that as yet there is no agreement on what Digital Libraries are and what functionality is associated with them. This results in a lack of interoperability and reuse of both content and technologies. This document attempts to put some order in the field for the benefit of its future advancement.

8.1 MOTIVATION

Digital Libraries constitute a relatively young scientific field, whose life spans roughly the last fifteen years.

Instrumental to the birth and growth of the field have been the funding opportunities generated by the 'Technology Enhanced Learning; Cultural Heritage' (formerly 'Cultural Heritage Applications') Unit of the Information Society Directorate-General of the European Commission and the 'Digital Library Initiatives' in the United States sponsored by the National Science Foundation and other agencies. Digital Libraries represent the meeting point of many disciplines and fields, including data management, information retrieval, library sciences, document management, information systems, the Web, image processing, artificial intelligence, human–computer interaction and digital curation. It was only natural that these first fifteen years were mostly spent on bridging some of the gaps between the disciplines (and the scientists serving each one), improvising on what 'Digital Library functionality' is supposed to be, and integrating solutions from each separate field into systems to support such functionality, sometimes the solutions being induced by novel requirements of Digital Libraries. These have been achieved through much exploratory work, primarily in the context of focused efforts devising specialised approaches to address particular aspects of Digital Library functionality.

8.2 THE DIGITAL LIBRARY UNIVERSE: A THREE-TIER FRAMEWORK

A Digital Library is an evolving organisation that comes into existence through a series of development steps that bring together all the necessary constituents. Below figure presents this process and indicates three distinct notions of 'systems' developed along the way forming a three-tier framework: Digital Library, Digital Library System, and Digital Library Management System. These correspond to three different levels of conceptualisation of the universe of Digital Libraries.

Digital Library (DL)

An organisation, which might be virtual, that comprehensively collects, manages and preserves for the long-term rich **digital content,** and offers to its **user** communities specialized **functionality** on that content, of measurable **quality** and according to codified **policies**.

Digital Library System (DLS)

A software system that is based on a defined (possibly distributed) **architecture** and provides all functionality required by a particular Digital Library. Users interact with a Digital Library through the corresponding Digital Library System.

Digital Library Management System (DLMS)

A generic software system that provides the appropriate software infrastructure both (i) to produce and administer a Digital Library System incorporating the suite of functionality considered fundamental for Digital Libraries, and (ii) to integrate additional software offering more refined, specialised or advanced functionality. A Digital Library Management System belongs to the class of 'system software'. As is the case in other related domains, such as operating systems, databases and user interfaces, DLMS software generation environments

Digital Library System Generator

A highly parameterised software system that encapsulates templates covering a broad range of functionalities, including a defined core suite of DL functionality as well as any advanced functionality that has been deemed appropriate to meet the needs of the specific application domain. Through an initialisation session, the appropriate parameters are set and configured; at the end of that session, an application is automatically generated, and this constitutes the Digital Library System ready for installation and deployment.

8.3 THE DIGITAL LIBRARY UNIVERSE: MAIN CONCEPTS

Despite the great variety and diversity of existing digital libraries, in reality only a limited range of concepts are defined by all systems as core functionalities. These concepts are identifiable in nearly every Digital Library currently in use. They serve as a starting point for any researcher who wants to study and understand the field, for any system designer and developer intending to construct a Digital Library, and for any content provider seeking to expose its content via digital library technologies. In this section, we identify these concepts and briefly discuss them. Six core concepts provide a foundation for Digital Libraries. Five of them appear in the definition of Digital Library: *Content, User, Functionality, Quality* and *Policy;* the sixth one emerges in the definition of Digital Library System: *Architecture.* All six concepts influence the Digital Library framework, as shown in Figure

FIG. 8.1

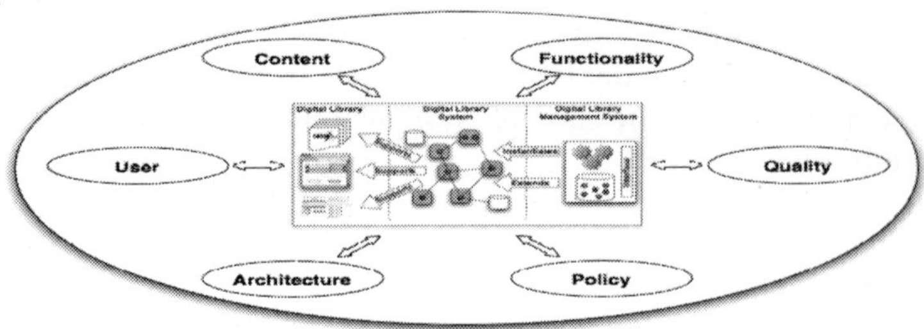

8.3.1 Content

The *Content* concept encompasses the data and information that the Digital Library handles and makes available to its users. It is composed of a set of information objects organised in collections. Content is an umbrella concept used to aggregate all forms of information objects that a Digital Library collects, manages and delivers. It encompasses the diverse range of information objects, including such resources as objects, annotations and metadata. For example, metadata have a central role in the handling and use of information objects, as they provide information critical to its syntactical, semantic and contextual interpretation.

8.3.2 User

The *User* concept covers the various actors (whether human or machine) entitled to interactwith Digital Libraries. Digital Libraries connect actors with information and support them in their ability to consume and make creative use of it to generate new information. User is an umbrella concept including all notions related to the representation and management of actor entities within a Digital Library. It encompasses such elements as the rights that actors have within the system and the profiles of the actors with characteristics that personalise the system's behaviour or represent these actors in collaborations.

8.3.3 Functionality

The *Functionality* concept encapsulates the services that a Digital Library offers to its different users, whether classes of users or individual users. While the general expectation is that DLs will be rich in capabilities and services, the bare minimum of functions would include such aspects as new information object registration, search and browse. Beyond that, the system seeks to manage the functions of the Digital Library to ensure that the functions reflect the particular needs of the Digital Library's community of users and/or the specific requirements relating to the Content it contains.

8.3.4 Quality

The *Quality* concept represents the parameters that can be used to characterise and evaluate the content and behaviour of a Digital Library. Quality can be associated not only with each class of content or functionality but also with specific information objects or services. Some of these parameters are objective in nature and can be measured automatically, whereas others are subjective in nature and can only be measured through user evaluations (e.g. focus groups).

8.3.5 Policy

The *Policy* concept represents the set or sets of conditions, rules, terms and regulations governing interaction between the

Digital Library and users, whether virtual or real. Examples of policies include acceptable user behaviour, digital rights management, privacy and confidentiality, charges to users, and collection delivery. Policies belong to different classes; for instance, not all policies are defined within the DL or the organisation managing it. The policy supports the distinction between extrinsic and intrinsic policies. The definition of new policies and re-definition of older policies will be a feature of digital libraries.

8.3.6 Architecture

The *Architecture* concept refers to the Digital Library System entity and represents a mapping of the functionality and content offered by a Digital Library on to hardware and software components. There are two primary reasons for having Architecture as a core concept: (i) Digital Libraries are often assumed to be among the most complex and advanced forms of information systems and (ii) interoperability across Digital Libraries is recognised as a substantial research challenge. A clear architectural framework for the Digital Library System offers ammunition in addressing both of these issues effectively.

Figure 8.2 puts in perspective the six main concepts of the Digital Library world. Among these, three are independent, i.e. their existence does not depend on the existence of a digital library. These are *Architecture,* representing the technological design on which the Digital Library System is based, *User,* representing the external humans or hardware interacting with the Digital Library, and *Content,* representing the material handled by the Digital Library. On top of these comes *Functionality,* representing primarily the means for connecting *User* to *Content,* i.e. all procedures, transformations, actions and interactions that bring *Content* to *User* or *vice versa.* Finally, operation of the Digital Library and activation of its *Functionality* are based on *Policy* and aim to achieve certain *Quality*.

The six core concepts (Content, User, Functionality, Quality, Policy and Architecture) that lie at the heart of the

FIG. 8.2

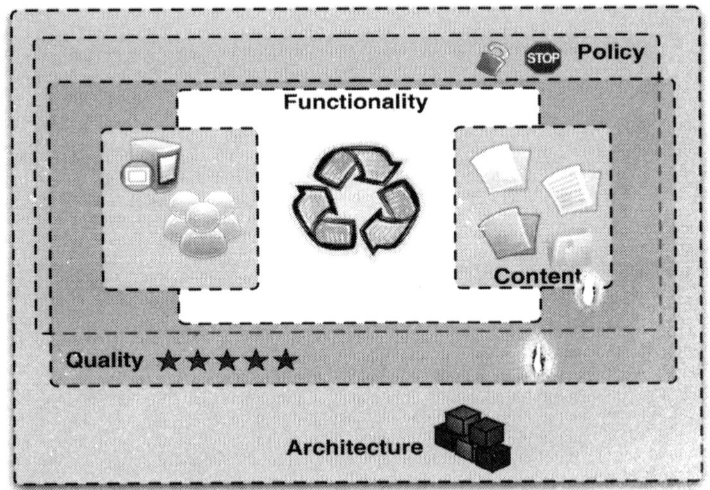

Digital Library universe need to be considered in conjuction with the four mai ways in which actors interact with digital library systems, as discussed in the next section.

8.4 THE DIGITAL LIBRARY UNIVERSE : THE MAIN ROLES OF ACTORS

We envisage actors interacting with digital library systems in foru different and complementary ways : DL End-users, DL Designers, DL System Administrators and DL Application Developers.Each role is primarily associated with one of the three 'systems' in the three-tier framework.

FIG. 8.3

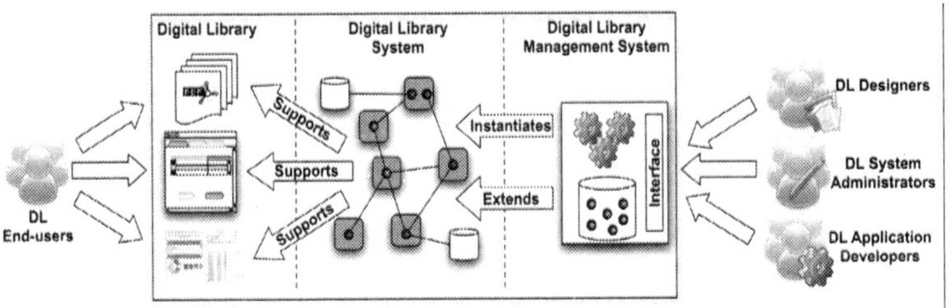

8.4.1 DL End-users

DL End-users exploit the DL functionality for the purpose of providing, consuming and managing the DL Content and some of its other constituents. They perceive the DL as a stateful entity serving their functional needs. The behaviour and output of the DL depend on the DL's state at the time a particular part of its functionality is activated. The state of the DL corresponds to the state of its *resources*, which, as we have seen above, consist of the collections of information objects managed by the DL, the set of authorised users, the DL's functionality and its set of policies. This state changes during the lifetime of the Digital Library according to the functionality activated by users and their inputs. DL Content Creators are the producers of the DL Content; they feed it with the resources, mainly information objects, to which other users of the DL will have access. This activity is (i) accomplished through the Functionality the DL provides, (ii) regulated by the Policies defined in the DL, and (iii) performed according to the Quality the DL must guarantee. Content Consumers are the purchasers of the DL Content; in reality, these users consume all the resources a DL makes available. In fact, they access Content: (i) through the Functionality the DL provides, (ii) in accordance with the Policies defined in the DL, and (iii) with the guarantee of Quality the DL declares. Librarians are End-users in charge of curating the DL Content. In fact, these actors have to curate all the resources forming the DL, e.g. establish the Policies.

8.4.2 DL Designers

DL Designers exploit their knowledge of the application semantic domain in order to define, customise and maintain the Digital Library so that it is aligned with the information and functional needs of its potential DL End-users. To perform this task, the DL Designers interact with the DLMS providing functional and content configuration parameters. Functional parameters instantiate aspects of the DL functionality that are to be perceived by the DL End-users, including the characteristics of the result set format, query language(s), user profile formats, and document/data model employed. Content configuration parameters specify third-party resources exploited by the specific DL, e.g. repositories of content, ontologies, classification schemas, authority files, and gazetteers that will be used to form the DL Content. The values of these parameters configure the way the DL will be presented to the DL End-users, as they determine the particular Digital Library System instance serving the Digital Library. Of course, these parameters need not necessarily be fixed for the entire lifetime of the DL; they may be reconfigured to enable the DL to respond to the evolving expectations of users and changes in all aspects from policies to content.

8.4.3 DL System Administrators

DL System Administrators select the software components needed to construct the Digital Library System. Their choice of elements reflects the expectations that DL End-users and DL Designers have for the Digital Library, as well as the equirements the available resources impose on the definition of the DL. DL System Administrators interact with the DLMS by providing architectural configuration parameters, such as the chosen software components and the selected hosting nodes. Their task is to identify the architectural configuration that best fits the DLS in order to ensure the highest level of quality of service. The value of the architectural configuration parameters can be changed over the DL lifetime. Changes of parameter configuration may result in the provision of different DL functionality and/or different levels of quality of service.

8.4.4 DL Application Developers

DL Application Developers develop the software components that will be used as constituents of the DLSs, to ensure that the appropriate levels and types of functionality are available.

8.4.5 Where are the Librarians?

The reader may be surprised that this Manifesto purports to cover the Digital Library world but none of the above-envisaged classes of actors is termed 'Librarian'. In fact, a kind of Enduser was termed as *Librarian* but this captures only one particular facet of Librarians playing a fundamental role in the Digital Library universe. Today, *Librarians* are a kind of actor spanning many of the envisaged roles, as demonstrated by the description provided. Because the DL End-user executes functionality for providing, consuming and managing the DL content, the model includes in this category the 'End-user Librarian', i.e. Librarians acting as cataloguers and curators in the Library world and those interfacing with and supporting the users of a Library.

End-user Librarians are the front end to Library clients; as the Digital Library world has no physical place that represents the DL, these actors interact with the other users via the 'system'. Because the DL Designer exploits her/his knowledge of the application semantic domain to define, customise and maintain the Digital Library, it is paired with the 'Digital Librarian', i.e. the chief librarian who decides the policies regulating the Library. Finally, the DL System Administrator is paired with the 'System Librarian', i.e. the Librarian with technical skills entitling her/him to manage the DL software system. Thus, even if none of the actors is termed 'Librarian', the Manifesto is capable of representing the various 'incarnations' a *Librarian* can assume. The four roles described above encompass the entire spectrum of actors interacting with digital libraries. Their models of the DL Universe are linked together in a hierarchical fashion, as shown in Figure. This hierarchy is a direct consequence of the above definitions, since DL End-users act on the Digital Library, whereas DL Designers, DL System Administrators and DL Application Developers operate on the DLS (through the mediation of a DLMS) and, consequently, on the DL as well. This inclusion relationship ensures that cooperating actors share a common vocabulary and knowledge. For instance, the DL End-user expresses requirements in terms of the DL model and, subsequently, the DL Designer understands these requirements and defines the DL accordingly.

FIG. 8.4
Hierarchy of Users' Views

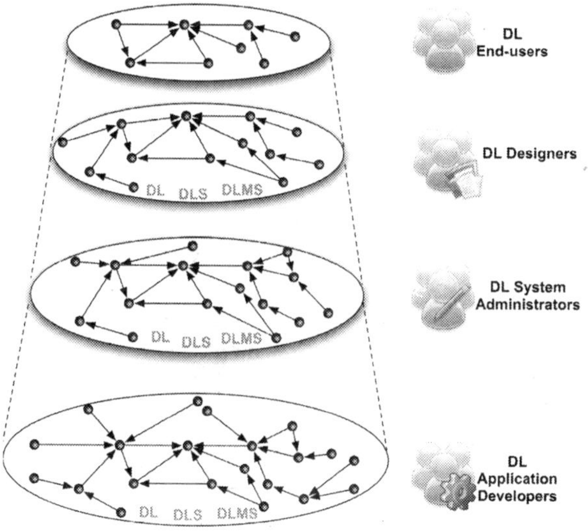

DL End-users

DL Designers

DL System Administrators

DL Application Developers

DL DLS DLMS

8.5 DIGITAL LIBRARY DEVELOPMENT FRAMEWORK

An explained earlier, the Digital Library universe is a complex world. Consequently, it is difficult to identify a single and fully-fledged model capable of capturing all the aspects needed to represent this universe in all the necessary scenarios. One of the scenarios in which such modelling activity is particularly important is the pattern leading to the development of concrete systems. This scenario is very broad, as being capable of capturing the peculiarities of an entity at a level of detail that allow developers to implement such an entity requires the capability to capture a comprehensive set of aspects that characterise the entity and thus can be reused in a plethora of other application domains, e.g. teaching, comparing existing systems. However, such a model may be difficult to use if it is not appropriately designed, i.e. tailored to address the specific needs of the audience for which it is designed. For this reason, we structured the model needed to capture the Digital Library universe and enabled it to implement its constituents in multiple elements which can be better represented in detail by introducing frameworks supporting different levels of abstraction.

FIG. 8.5

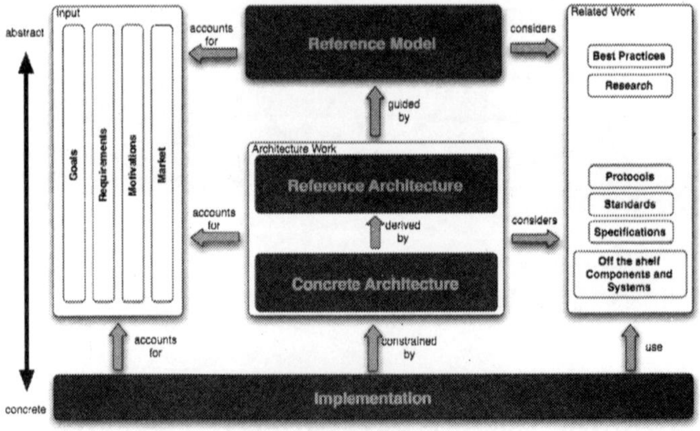

More specifically, the elements constituting the Development Framework are :

- *Reference Model*—'A Reference Model consists of a minimal set of unifying concepts, axioms and relationships within a particular problem domain, and is independent of specific standards, technologies, implementations, or other concrete details'. Digital libraries need a corresponding Reference Model in order to consolidate the diversity of existing approaches into a cohesive and consistent whole, to offer a mechanism for enabling the comparison of different Digital Library systems, to provide a common basis for communication within the Digital Library community, and to help focus further advancement.

- *Reference Architecture*—The Reference Architecture is an architectural design pattern indicating an abstract solution that implements the concepts and relationships identified in the Reference Model. There may be more than one Reference Architecture that addresses how to design digital library systems built on the Reference Model. For example, we might have one Reference Architecture for DLSs supporting DLs constructed by federating local resources and multiple organisations, and another one for personal DLs or for specialised applications.
- *Concrete Architecture*—At this level, the Reference Architecture is realised by replacing the mechanisms envisaged in the Reference Architecture with concrete standards and specifications. For example, a Concrete Architecture may specify that the run-time environment deployed on the hosting nodes will be CORBA or the Web Services Application Framework, and that a number of specific communicating Web Services will implement the Search functional component.

8.6 CONCLUSION

This article has presented the core parts of *The Digital Library Manifesto* produced by members of the DELOS Network of Excellence on Digital Libraries to be used as a springboard for future foundational research and development in the domain of Digital Libraries.

The Digital Library Manifesto is accompanied by two other works currently available in their first release as a DELOS deliverable introducing the DL Reference Model and a DLS Reference Architecture. We hope that these documents will provoke discussion and debate within the digital library community that will promote their improvement. Clearly, diversity of needs among different digital library "systems" will continue to introduce new concepts that will require incorporation into the Reference Model and in the Reference Architectures. Hence, these documents should be considered as first versions of otherwise dynamic documents that will keep evolving, having the *Manifesto* as a firm foundation.

9

Electronic Library

9.0 INTRODUCTION

Performance indicators provide library managers with a standard and manageable method of measuring the library's performance as well as allowing benchmarking and comparison between libraries. Electronic library services have been increasing in importance in terms of the percentage of the library budget being spent on them and in terms of the ease of access that they provide to users. However, to date no standard method has been available for evaluating how this important section of library services is performing and whether value for money is being achieved. The term 'library' is used throughout but can be taken to refer to an information service irrespective of its title.

The feedback received and the testing of the PIs showed that while this initial set was very useful, further revision of the PI list was required. Some PIs were felt to be too demanding of staff time in relation to the value of the information gleaned. Others were felt to be somewhat confusing and difficult to calculate. In many cases, the data required simply wasn't available from many of the electronic library services currently in use in libraries.

The revised set of performance indicators, together with a definition of terms used is listed below. The full definition and collection methodology for each PI is available on the project The final phase of the project will further refine these performance indicators to reflect feedback received; comments are therefore welcome even at this late stage of the project, directly to the author or through the project Web site.

User satisfaction with each electronic library service and electronic library services generally would provide enhanced qualitative management information, in particular when considered in conjunction with PIs such as numbers 2 and 5 below. By considering pairs of PIs together in this way the manager can elicit even more valuable information. For example, the cost per session of a particular service considered in conjunction with the number of documents downloaded per session can give a better indication of value for money than has been available heretofore.

9.1 PERFORMANCE INDICATORS

1. Percentage of the population reached by electronic library services.
2. Number of sessions on each electronic library service per member of the target population.
3. Number of remote sessions on electronic library services per member of the population to be served.
4. Number of documents and entries (records) downloaded per session for each electronic library service.
5. Cost per session for each electronic library service.
6. Cost per document or entry (record) downloaded for each electronic library service.
7. Percentage of information requests submitted electronically.
8. Library computer workstation use rate.
9. Number of library computer workstation hours available per member of the population to be served.

10. Rejected sessions as a percentage of total attempted sessions.
11. Percentage of total acquisitions expenditure spent on acquisition of electronic library resources.
12. Number of attendances at formal electronic library service training sessions per member of the target population.

9.2 LIBRARY AUTOMATION SOFTWARE PACKAGE-SOFTWARE MODULES

9.1.0 Introduction

The Electronic Library is a state-of-the-art library automation software program. Library automation for school library automation or church library automation is easy with this program. Library software has so many useful capabilities. It is a must, especially for a small school, college library and district library. And a computer background is not a pre-requesite to use this library automation software.

Software package for Libraries is a full-featured database system designed for small libraries. You can use the software to keep track of all types of books, magazines, videos, CDs and other media. For each item you can track title, author, subject, publisher, copyright year, date received, cost, image, value, minimum desired quantity, current quantity, ISBN, supplier, location, notes and much more. You can also record a loan history for each item, and you can generate reports showing you which items are overdue. The software also supports most barcode readers and can automatically generate and print barcodes. In addition, you can also use your barcode reader to easily jump to items in your database. The software features advanced reporting, graph generation, data export, a powerful search engine, full customization, optional web publishing and more.

9.3 SOFTWARE FEATURES

- **Easy to learn** user interface, designed for **quick** data entry.
- Multiple File Support.

- Large item capacity in each file.
- Advanced multi-level categorization system with customizable pull down menus to speed data entry.
- Keep track of title, author, subject, publisher, copyright year, date received, cost, image, value, minimum desired quantity, current quantity, ISBN, supplier, location, notes.
- Rich text format detail notes area for each item in your database.
- Feature checklist for each database item.
- Data area for recording **loan history**.
- Single step **overdue item reports**.
- **Barcode** generation, printing and scanning.
- Impressive 3-Dimensional Graphs showing you how your collection break downs.
- Powerful Search Features that allow you to easily retrieve information from your database.
- Ability to sort your data by almost any field in the database.
- Multiple image support with image enhancement and printing features.
- An album View where you can view different page scans in your database side by side.
- A Spreadsheet view where you can quickly browse through your database.
- An HTML Report Generator so you can post your database to your web site
- Detailed Online Help file.
- Ability to customize field names and drop down menu options to suite your individual needs.
- Ability to export primary data fields to CSV format (can be read by Excel and Access).
- Ability to scan in images.

9.4 SAMPLE SCREENS FROM WIL TECH SOFTWARE PACKAGE

The Electronic Library may be configured to meet the needs of any library. All reports bear the name of the orgranization entered here. The Accession number prefix

FIG. 9.1

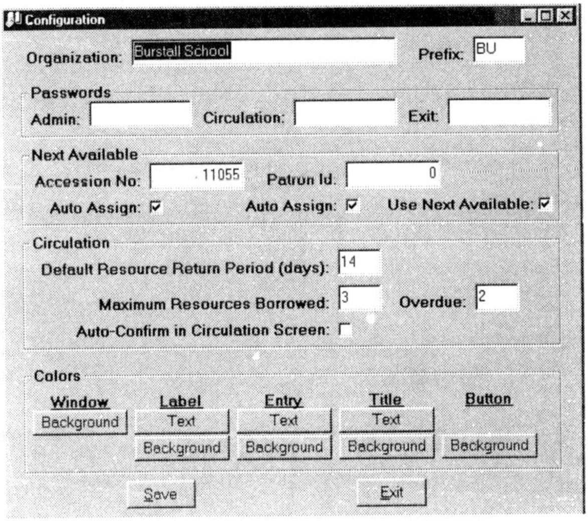

identifies the library to which resources belong. Administrative activities are protected by password. Accession and Patron Id. numbers are assigned by the computer. Maximum resources borrowed and overdue may be set to warn the librarian of the number resources patrons have out and/or overdue. Buttons at the bottom may be used to set various colors on the screen.

FIG. 9.2

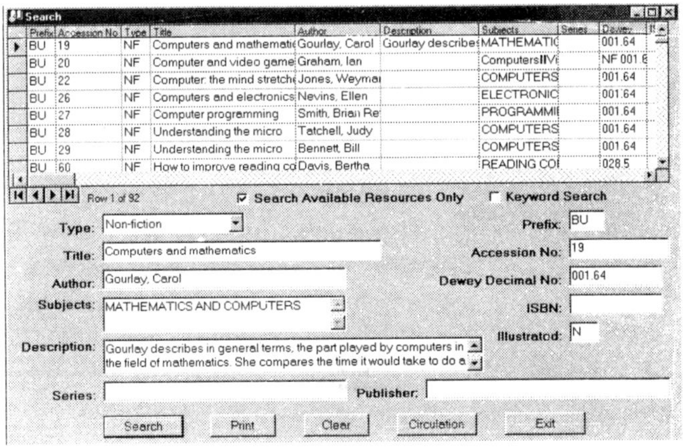

Take 'File', then 'Search' to bring up the screen below. Any search string may be entered into any field. A 'keyword' search will scan subjects and titles for the search string. Results are shown in the top window. Details of the record selected in the top window are shown below. Taking [Print] will send the list to the printer.

FIG. 9.3

Resource

Prefix: BU Accession No: 1 Status: Borrowed Last Activity: 1994/12/27

Type: Non-fiction Dewey: NF 001 Nus

Subjects: Animals Cats ISBN: ISBN [Add]

Illustrated: ☑ [Delete]

Author: Nussbaum, Hedda

Title: Charlie Brown's book of questions & answers [Save]

Description: This is the story of a young lad who has all the answers to all of the questions most often asked by school age children. The answers

[Borrow]

Series: Charlie Brown Copyright: 1976 [Return]

Publisher: Publisher Cost: 24.95

Location: Location Purchased: [Status]

Pages: 235 Bibliography - Pages: 232 to 234

Patron Id: Andrea Lippert Date: 1993/10/26

[Find] [First] [Prior] [Next] [Last] [Exit]

Take 'File', then 'Resources' to bring up the resources screen. It is here that resources are cataloged, resource records are modified or deleted. Status may be changed from 'Active' (available), to 'Inactive' (presumed lost), to 'Reserve' (not to be removed from library). Circulation may also be handled from here.

FIG. 9.4

December 21, 2003

Burstall School
Overdue Resource List
From 1992/01/01 to 2003/12/31

Page:

Prefix	Accession No	Borrowed	Due	Days Past	Name of Borrower	Title	Author
Grade 2							
BU	6,701	1993/12/21	1994/01/04	3638	Aaron Krein	Rivers and river life	Macdonald Educa
BU	2,465	1993/10/18	1993/11/01	3702	Andrea Baron	Renaissance	Hale, John R.
BU	160	2002/11/26	2002/12/09	377	Andrea Baron	Getting along with your family	Naylor, Phyllis
BU	6,012	1993/12/06	1993/12/20	3663	Derick Mason	No fighting no biting!	Minarik, Else Ho
BU	1,003	2003/09/24	2003/10/08	74	George Testingagain	Born free vol.2	Adamson, Joy
BU	6,700	1993/12/21	1994/01/04	3638	Lance Arthurs	The postman	Macdonald Educa
BU	11,132	2000/09/18	2000/10/02	1175	Michael Wuerfel		
Grade 3							
BU	446	2000/09/17	2000/10/01	1176	Brett Fauth	Christmas around the world	Hooper, Van B.
BU	447	2000/09/17	2000/10/01	1176	Brett Fauth	Nomads of the world	Breeden, Robert
BU	464	2000/09/17	2000/09/29	1178	Brett Fauth	World bk.ency.country sup.vol.	Field Enterpris
BU	5,600	1993/12/21	1994/01/04	3638	Carmen Ressler	The ball book	Hillert, Margare
BU	462	2000/09/17	2000/09/29	1178	Carmen Ressler	World bk ency country sup vol	Field Enterpris
BU	13	2002/10/27	2002/11/10	406	Cody Jassman	Kids guide to home computers	Cohen, Daniel
Grade 4							
BU	680	2000/09/17	2000/10/01	1176	Amy Krein	Black stallion returns	Farley, Walter

All reports appear first on the screen. The size of the report window may be set to anything from 25% to 400%. Reports set to 'page width' (fit exactly on the screen) are usually 87%. Clicking the printer icon sends the report to the printer.

FIG. 9.5

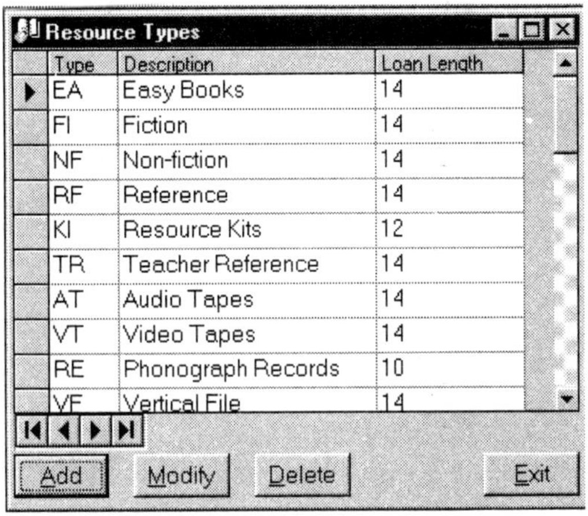

Resource Types

Type	Description	Loan Length
EA	Easy Books	14
FI	Fiction	14
NF	Non-fiction	14
RF	Reference	14
KI	Resource Kits	12
TR	Teacher Reference	14
AT	Audio Tapes	14
VT	Video Tapes	14
RE	Phonograph Records	10
VF	Vertical File	14

Add Modify Delete Exit

Taking 'File', then 'Resource Types' shows the following screen. Any number of resource types may be added here or existing ones deleted. The loan period set here raises the overdue flag. A different loan period may be set for each resource type.

Data Tracker
Demco
Wil-Tech
e-Granthalaya, etc.

9.5 SOME MARKET AVAILABLE LIBRARY SOFTWARE PACKAGES

Data Tracker
Demco
Wil-Tech
e-Granthalaya, etc.

Glossary

access delay

The time a network interface waits before it can access a shared network.

Acknowledgement

A short message returned to inform a sender that data has arrived at its intended destination.

Active document

A World Wide Web document that is a computer program. After downloading an active document, the browser runs the program on the user's computer. The active document can change the display continuously. See dynamic document, static document, and URL.

Adaptive retransmission

The ability of a transport protocol to change its retransmission timer continuously to accommodate variations in internet delay. TCP is the best known protocol that uses adaptive retransmission.

address mask

A 32-bit value that specifies the bits of an IP address that correspond to a network and a subnet. Address bits not covered by the mask correspond to the host portion. Also called a subnet mask.

address resolution

The mapping from one address to another, usually from a high-level address (e.g., an IP address) to a low-level address (e.g., an Ethernet address).

ADSL (Asymmetric Digital Subscriber Line)

A technology to deliver digital information at high-speed over the same twisted pair wiring used to deliver telephone service. The downstream bit rate is higher than the upstream rate because most subscribers retrieve much more information than they send.

anonymous FTP

Access to an FTP server using the login name *anonymous* and the password *guest*. Not all FTP servers permit anonymous FTP.

APCM (Adaptive Pulse Code Modulation)

A scheme for digital encoding of audio in which successive values represent differ-ences in the sampled wave instead of absolute values. See PCM.

API **(Application Program Interface)**

The set of procedures a computer program can call to access a particular service. The procedures a program uses to access network protocols is known as a network API.

applet

The computer program that comprises an active World Wide Web document. An applet is written in a programming language such as Java.

AppleTalk

A set of network protocols developed and sold by Apple Computer Corporation.

ARP (Address Resolution Protocol)

The protocol a computer uses to map an IP address into a hardware address. A computer that invokes ARP broadcasts a request to which the target computer replies.

ASCII (American Standard Code for Information Interchange)

A standard that assigns unique values to 128 characters, including upper and lower case letters, digits, punctuation, and control characters. Details can be found in Appendix 2. See EBCDIC.

ASN.1 (Abstract Syntax Notation.1)

A standard for representing data. The SNMP protocol uses ASN.l to represent object names.

asynchronous

Characteristic of any communication system in which the sender can transmit data without warning. The receiver must be prepared to accept data at any time. See synchronous.

ATM (Asynchronous Transfer Mode)

A connection-oriented technology defined by the ITU and the ATM Forum. At the lowest level, ATM sends aU data in fixed cells with *48* octets of data per cell.

AUI (Attachment Unit Interface)

The type of connector used with thick wire Ethernet. An AUI connection exists between a computer and an Ethernet transceiver.

AWT (Abstract Window Toolkit)

A library of graphics procedures used with the Java language to manipulate windows on a bit-mapped display. At various times, the designers have expanded AWT to Alternative Window Toolkit and Applet Widget Toolkit.

B channel (Bearer channel)

The term telephone companies use to denote a channel configured to handle a voice telephone circuit. ISDN includes B channel service. See D channel.

Bandwidth

A measure of the capacity of a transmission system. Bandwidth is measured in Hertz.

Base header

The required header found at the beginning of an IPv6 datagram.

baseband technology

The term used to describe a networking technology that uses a small part of the electromagnetic spectrum and sends only one signal at a time over the underlying medium. Most LANs use baseband signaling (e.g., Ethernet and FDDI). See broadband technology.

baud

The number of changes in a signal per second. Each change can encode one or more bits of information.

best-effort

Characteristic of any network system that makes a best attempt to deliver data, but does not guarantee delivery. Many networks use the best-effort approach.

bidding

A technique protocols use for dynamic address configuration. A computer selects an address at random, and broadcasts a message to determine whether the address is in use. Alternative schemes use servers to manage addresses. See DHCP.

binary exponential backoff

The scheme used by computers on an Ethernet following a collision. Each computer doubles the time it waits after each successive collision.

bits per second

The rate at which data can be transmitted across a network. The number of bits per second may differ from the baud rate because more than one bit can be encoded in a single baud.

BNC connector

The type of connector used with thin wire Ethernet.

BOOTP (BOOTstrap Protocol)

A protocol that a computer uses when it first starts to obtain information needed to configure the protocol software. BOOTP uses IP and UDP to broadcast a request and receive a response before IP has been completely configured.

BRI (Basic Rate Interface)

The ISDN service that provides two B channels plus a data channel. BRI is suitable for small businesses. See PRI.

bridge

A hardware device that connects two LAN segments and copies frames from one to the other. Most bridge hardware uses physical addresses to leam which computers attach to which segments so the bridge can avoid copying frames unless needed.

broadband technology

The term used to describe a networking technology that uses a large part of the electromagnetic spectrum to achieve higher throughput rates. Usually broadband systems employ frequency division multiplexing to allow multiple, independent communications to proceed simultaneously over a single underlying medium. See baseband technology.

broadcast

A form of delivery in which one copy of a packet is delivered to each computer on a network. See cluster, multicast, and unicast.

broadcast address

A special address that causes the underlying system to deliver a copy of a packet to all computers on a network.

browser

A computer program that accesses and displays information from the World Wide Web. A browser contains multiple application programs, and uses an object's name to determine which application should be used to access the object. See URL.

bus topology

A network architecture in which all computers attach to a shared medium, often a single cable. The bus architecture is mainly used for Local Area Networks.

byte stuffing

A protocol technique in which data is changed by inserting additional bytes to distinguish between data values and packet control fields.

cable modem

A modem used to send digital information over the coaxial cables used for cable television.

carrier

The basic signal transmitted across a network. A carrier is modulated (i.e., changed) to encode data.

category 5 cable

A type of wiring needed for twisted pair Ethernet. The electrical characteristics of category 5 make it less susceptible to electrical interference than lower categories.

CATV (Community Antenna Television)

The name applied to cable television systems. CATV technology uses frequency division multiplexing to propagate multiple television channels over a single cable simultaneously. See cable modem.

CCITT (Consultative Committee on International Telephone and Telegraph) The former name of the ITU.

CDDI (Copper Distributed Data Interconnection) FDDI technology adapted to run over copper wire.

cell

A small, fixed size packet (e.g., ATM networks send 48-octet cells).

CGI (Common Gateway Interface)

A technology used to create dynamic World Wide Web documents. CGI programs run on the server computer.

checksum

A value used to verify that data is not corrupted during transmission. The sender computes a checksum by adding the binary values of the data, and transmits the result in a packet with the data. A sender computes a checksum over the data received, and compares the value to the checksum in the packet. See CRC.

client

When two programs communicate over a network, a client is the one that initiates communication, while the program that waits to be contacted is a server. A given program can act as a server for one service and a client for another.

client-server paradigm

The method of interaction used when two application programs communicate over a network. A server application waits at a known address, and a client application contacts the server.

cluster

A form of addressing used by IPv6 in which a set of computers is assigned one address; a datagram sent to the address can be delivered to any one of the computers in the set. See broadcast, multicast, and unicast.

coaxial cable

A type of cable used for computer networks as well as for cable television. The name arises from the structure in which a metal shield surrounds a center wire. The shield protects the signal on the inner wire from electrical interference.

collision

An event that occurs on a CSMA/CD network when two stations attempt to transmit simultaneously. The signals interfere with each other, forcing the two stations to back off and try again.

colon hexadecimal notation

The syntactic notation used to express an IPv6 address.

congestion

A condition in which each packet sent through a network experiences excessive delay because the network is overrun with packets. Unless protocol software detects congestion and reduces the rate at which packets are sent, a network can experience congestion collapse.

connection-oriented

A characteristic of network systems that require a pair of computers to establish a connection before sending data. Connection-oriented networks are analogous to a telephone system in which a call must be placed and answered before communication can begin. See connectionless.

connectionless

A characteristic of network systems that allow a computer to send data to any other computer at any time. Connectionless networks are analogous to a postal system in which each letter carries the address of the recipient; letters can be sent at any time. See connection-oriented.

CRC (Cyclic Redundancy Check)

A value used to verify that data is not corrupted during transmission. The sender computes a CRC and transmits the result in a packet with the data. A receiver computes the CRC over the data received, and compares the value to the CRC in the packet. A CRC is more complex to compute than a checksum, but can detect more transmission errors.

CSMA (Carrier Sense Multiple Access)

The technique used with bus architecture networks in which computers attached to the common bus check for the presence of a carrier before transmitting.

CSMA/CD (Carrier Sense Multiple Access with Collision Detection)

A CSMA network that has the capability to detect errors that result when multiple stations transmit simultaneously. See collision.

D channel

The term telephone companies use to denote a channel configured to handle data. ISDN includes D channel service. See B channel.

DB-25

A 25-pin connector often used with serial lines.

default route

A wild-card entry in a routing table. The routing software follows the default route if the table does not contain an explicit route to the destination.

delay-bandwidth product

A measure of a network that specifies the amount of data that will be present in the network between the sender and receiver.

demodulator

A device that accepts a modulated carrier wave and extracts the information used to modulate it. See modem.

demultiplex

A general concept that refers to separating information received over a common communication channel into its original components. Demultiplexing occurs both in hardware (i.e., electrical signals can be demultiplexed) and in software (i.e., protocol software can demultiplex incoming messages and pass each to the correct application program). See multiplex.

destination address

An address in a packel that specifies the ultimate destination to which the packet is sent. In a hardware frame, the destination address must be a hardware address. In an IP datagram, the destination address must be an IP address.

DHCP (Dynamic Host Configuration Protocol)

A protocol that computers use to obtain configuration information. DHCP allows a computer to be assigned an IP address without requiring a manager to configure information about the computer in a server's database.

dialup modem

A modem that uses the dialup telephone network to communicate. Dialup modems must be able to dial or answer a telephone call and use an audible tone as a carrier wave.

digital signature

Data encrypted in such a way that the receiver can verify the identity of the sender.

Dijkstras algorithm

An algorithm for computing shortest paths in a graph. Routing protocols use Dijkstra's algorithm to compute optimal routes.

directed broadcast

A broadcast to all computers on a remote network achieved by sending a single copy of the packet to the remote network and broadcasting the packet when it arrives. TCP/IP supports directed broadcast.

distance-vector

An algorithm that routers use to compute optimal routes to each destination. Periodically, each router receives routing information from neighboring routers. A router replaces a current route if a lower cost route becomes available. See link-state and SPF.

distributed spanning tree

An algorithm that bridges use when they boot to detect and break cycles.

DIX Ethernet (Digital Intel Xerox Ethernet)

A term used for the original Ethernet because the standard was developed jointly by the three companies.

DNS (Domain Name System)

The automated system used to translate computer names into equivalent IP addresses. A DNS server responds to a query by looking up the name and returning the address. See domain.

domain

A part of the computer naming hierarchy used in the Internet. For example, commercial organizations have names registered under the *.com* domain.

dotted decimal notation

The syntactic notation used to express a 32-bit IPv4 address. Each octet is written in decimal with a period separating octets.

DS-1.DS-3

The designations that telephone companies use for the speeds of popular point-to-point digital circuits. DS-1 denotes 1.544 Mbps and DS-3 denotes 44.736 Mbps. See TI,T3.

DSU/CSU (Data Service Unit/Channel Service Unit)

An electronic device that connects a leased digital data circuit with computer equipment. The DSU/CSU translates between the digital format used by the telephone companies and that used by the computer industry. See modem.

dynamic document

A computer program associated with a World Wide Web document that can generate a document on demand. When a browser requests a dynamic document, the server runs the program and sends the output to the browser. A dynamic document program can generate different output for each request. See active document, static document, and URL.

e-mail (electronic mail)

A popular application in which a user or computer sends a memo to one or more recipients.

EBCDIC (Extended Binary Coded Decimal Interchange Code)

A standard that assigns unique values to 256 characters, including upper and lower case letters, digits, punctuation, and control characters. See ASCII.

echo reply

A message used for testing and debugging. An ICMP echo reply is returned in answer to an ICMP echo request message. The ping program receives echo replies. See echo request.

echo request

A message used for testing and debugging. The ping program sends ICMP echo request messages to elicit echo replies. See echo reply.

encapsulation

The technique in which information to be sent is placed inside the data area of a packet or frame. A packet from one protocol can be encapsulated in another (e.g., ICMP can be encapsulated in IP).

encryption key

The short value used when encrypting data to guarantee privacy. In some encryption schemes, the receiver must use the same key to decrypt the data. Other schemes use a pair of keys—one to encrypt and a different key to decrypt.

end-to-end

Characteristic of any protocol or function that operates on the original source and ultimate destination, but not on intermediate computers (e.g., not on routers).

endpoint address

A generic term for any address assigned to a computer that can be used as a destination address. For example, an IP address is one type of endpoint address.

Ethernet

A popular Local Area Network technology that uses a shared bus topology and CSMA/CD access. Basic Ethernet operates at 10 Mbps, Fast Ethernet operates at 100 Mbps, and Gigabit Ethernet operates at 1000 Mbps (i.e., 1 Gbps).

even parity

A parity bit added to a unit of data, usually each character, to make the number of bits even. A receiver checks the parity to determine whether data has been corrupted during transmission. See odd parity.

extension header

An optional header used in the IPv6 protocol.

exterior switch

A switch in a packet switched network to which host computers connect. See interior switch.

Fast Ethernet

A version of Ethernet technology that operates at 100 Mbps.

FDDI (Fiber Distributed Data Interconnect)

A Local Area Network technology that uses fiber optics to interconnect stations in a ring topology.

feeder circuit

A term used with cable television that refers to the wiring between a neighborhood concentration point and individual subscribers. A feeder circuit is less than two miles long. See trunk circuit.

fiber

Abbreviation for optical fiber.

fiber modem

A modem that uses modulated light waves to provide digital communication. A fiber modem uses light emitting diodes or lasers to transmit light. See optical fiber.

flow control

A protocol mechanism that allows a receiver to control the rate at which a sender transmits data. Flow control makes it possible for a receiver running on a low-speed computer to accept data from a high-speed computer without being overrun.

forward

See store and forward.

fragment

A small IP datagram produced by fragmentation.

fragmentation

The technique IP uses to divide a large datagram into smaller datagrams called fragments. The ultimate destination reassembles the fragments. See reassembly.

frame

The form of a packet that the underlying hardware accepts and delivers.

Frame Relay

A Wide Area Network technology that provides connection-oriented service.

framing error

An error that occurs on asynchronous serial lines in which the receiver does noi detect a valid frame (usually a character). Differences in the sender's and receiver's baud rate can cause framing errors.

frequency division multiplexing

A general multiplexing technique that allows multiple senders to transmit across a common medium. Because each sender uses a different frequency, multiple senders can transmit at the same time without interference.

FTP (File Transfer Protocol)

A protocol used to transfer a complete file from one computer to another.

FTTC (Fiber To The Curb)

A technology proposed as a replacement for the existing cable television infrastructure that uses fiber optic trunks and a combination of coaxial cable and twisted pair to each subscriber.

full-duplex transmission

A communication between two computers in which data can flow in both directions at the same time. Full-duplex transmission requires two independent channels, one for data in each direction. See half-duplex transmission.

Gbps (Giga bits per second)

A unit of data transfer equal to *1024* Mbps.

GEO (Geostationary Earth Orbit)

A height for communication satellites that causes their orbit to match the rotation of the earth (approximately 36,000 kilometers or 20,000 miles). Also called Geosynchronous Earth Orbit.

GIF (Graphics Interchange Format)

A standard format for storing a graphics image. GIF images are especially popular on the World Wide Web.

Gigabit Ethernet

A version of Ethernet technology that operates at 1000 Mbps (i.e., 1 Gbps).

half-duplex transmission

A communication between two computers in which data can flow in only one direction at a given time. Half-duplex transmission requires less hardware than full-duplex transmission because a single, shared physical medium can be used for all communication. See full-duplex transmission.

hardware address

The address assigned to a computer that attaches to a network. A frame sent from one computer to another must contain the recipient's hardware address. A hardware address is also called a physical address or a MAC address.

HDSL (High-rate Digital Subscriber Line)

A technology developed by the phone companies to provide high speed digital service over local loop wiring. See ADSL.

Hertz

A unit of measure equal to an oscillation per second. Hardware bandwidth is measured in multiples of Hertz.

HFC (Hybrid Fiber Coax)

A replacement for the existing cable television infrastructure that uses optical fiber trunks with coaxial cable connections to each subscriber and provides 2-way digital information transfer in addition to television signals. See cable modem.

hierarchical addressing

An addressing scheme in which part of an address gives information about the location. For example, a telephone number is hierarchical because it begins with an area code followed by an exchange.

homepage

A document stored on a World Wide Web server that is the starting point for obtaining information about a particular individual, company, group, or topic. A homepage can contain pointers to additional pages of related information or to homepages for other topics.

hop count

A number in a protocol header that determines how many intermediate machines a packet visits. Protocols like IP require the sender to specify a maximum hop count; doing so prevents a packet from traveling around a routing loop forever.

hop limit

A synonym for hop count that is used by IPv6.

host

An end-user's computer connected to a network. In an internet, each computer is classified as a host or a router.

HTML (HyperText Markup Language)

The source form used for documents on the World Wide Web. HTML embeds commands that determine formatting along with the text to be displayed (e.g., to move to a new line or indent text).

HTTP (HyperText Transport Protocol)

The protocol used to transport a World Wide Web page from one computer to another.

hub

An electronic device that implements a network. Computers connected to a hub can communicate as if they attach to a network.

hypermedia

A set of documents in which a given document can contain text, graphics, video and audio clips as well as embedded references to other documents. World Wide Web pages are hypermedia documents.

hypertext

A set of documents in which a given document can contain text as well as embedded references to other documents. See hypermedia.

IANA (Internet Assigned Number Authority)

The organization responsible for assigning numbers that the TCP/IP protocols use. For example, IANA assigns numeric values used in protocol header fields.

IBM Token Ring

A Local Area Network technology developed by IBM Corporation that uses ring to^ pology.

ICMP (Internet Control Message Protocol)

The protocol that IP uses to report errors and exceptions. ICMP also includes informational messages used by programs like ping.

interior switch

A switch in a packet switched network that only connects to other packet switches, but not to host computers. See exterior switch.

internet

A set of networks connected by routers that are configured to pass traffic among any computers attached to networks in the set. Most internets use TCP/IP protocols.

Internet

The global internet that uses TCP/IP protocols.

Internet address

See IP address.

Internet firewall

A security mechanism placed at the connection between networks in an organization and networks outside the organization. The firewall restricts access to the organization's computers and services.

Internet reference model

A 5-layer model that describes the conceptual purpose of protocols in the TCP/IP protocol suite.

IP (Internet Protocol)

The protocol that defines both the format of packets used on a TCP/IP Internet and the mechanism for routing a packet to its destination.

IP address

A 32-bit address assigned to a computer that uses TCP/IP protocols. The sender must know the IP address of the destination computer before sending a packet.

IP datagram

The form of a packet sent across a TCP/IP internet. Each datagram has a header that identifies both the sender and receiver followed by data.

IPng (Internet Protocol—the Next Generation)

The generic name used during early discussions of a new protocol to succeed IPv4. Researchers proposed several possible protocols for IPng. See IPv6.

IPv4 (Internet Protocol Version 4)

The version of IP currently used in the Internet. IPv4 uses 32-bit addresses.

IPv6 (Internet Protocol Version 6)

A specific protocol that has been chosen by the IETF as a successor to IPv4. IPv6 uses 128-bit addresses.

IPX (Internet Packet exchange)

A protocol family defined by Novell Corporation. IPX is not related to IP.

ISDN (integrated Services Digital Network)

A digital communication service defined by the telephone companies. Many experts think that high price and low bit rates make ISDN unattractive.

ISO (International Organization for Standardization)

The standards organization best known for having proposed the 7-layer reference model early in the history of data networking.

ISP (Internet Service Provider)

A commercial organization that provides its subscribers with access to the Internet.

ITU (International Telecommunications Union)

The organization that controls standards for telephone systems. The ITU also standardizes a few network technologies (e.g., ATM).

Java

A programming language defined by Sun Microsystems for use in active World Wide Web documents. Java programs are compiled into a bytecode representation. After a browser loads a Java program, the program runs locally to control the display.

JavaScript

An interpretative language used for active World Wide Web documents. Because they are kept in source form, JavaScript programs can be integrated with text in a World Wide Web page.

jitter

A term that refers to the amount of variation in delay that a network introduces. A network with zero jitter takes exactly the same amount of time to transfer each packet, while a network with high jitter takes much longer to deliver some packets than others. Jitter is important when sending audio or video, which must arrive at regular intervals.

Kbps (Kilo bits per second)

A unit of data transfer equal to *1024* bits per second.

LAN (Local Area Network)

A network that uses technology designed to span a small geographic area. For example, an Ethernet is a LAN technology suitable for use in a single building. LANs have lower propagation delay than WANs. See WAN.

layering model

A conceptual framework used to explain the purpose and interaction among a set of protocols. Layering is primarily beneficial to protocol designers; once implemented, protocols can be used without understanding layering.

LEO (Low Earth Orbit)

A height for communication satellites in which one orbit takes approximately 90 minutes.

link-state

An algorithm that routers use to compute optimal routes to each destination. Each router receives information about the status of network links, and uses the information in a shortest-path computation. See Dijkstra's algorithm, SPF, and distance-vector.

LLC (Logical Link Control)

Part of the IEEE LLC/SNAP header used to identify the type of a packet. The entire header is *8* octets, with the LLC portion occupying the first three. See SNAP.

local loop

A term that telephone companies use to refer to the wiring between the central office and a subscriber (e.g., an individual business or residence). A variety of technologies have been developed to provide high speed digital services over existing local loop wiring. See ADSL.

locality of reference

A term used to express the idea that communication tends to follow patterns. Spatial locality of reference means that a computer is more likely to communicate with a nearby computer than a distant computer, and temporal locality of reference means that a computer is more likely to communicate with the same computer repeatedly than to communicate with a new computer each time.

LocalTalk

A Local Area Network technology developed by Apple Computer Corporation that uses a bus topology. LocalTalk uses AppleTalk protocols.

long-haul network

Synonym for Wide Area Network.

loopback address

A special address that is used for testing or debugging. A packet sent to the loop-back address is not transmitted over a network, but is returned by the protocol system as if it arrived over the network.

mail exploder

A program used to forward e-mail messages. A mail exploder consults a database to determine how to handle each message. The name arises because a mail exploder may send copies of a message to multiple recipients if the database specifies many recipients for the address.

mesh network

A network architecture in which a computer has a point-to-point connection to other computers). Full mesh networks, in which each pair of computers is directly connected offer the highest throughput but are uncommon because they are expensive and difficult to change. See bus topology and ring topology.

Mbps (Mega bits per second)

A unit of data transfer equal to *1024* Kbps.

MIB (Management Information Base)

A set of named items that an SNMP agent understands. To monitor or control a remote computer, a manager must fetch or store values to MIB variables.

MIME (Multipurpose Internet Mail Extensions)

A mechanism that allows nontext data to be sent in a standard Internet e-mail message. A MIME sender encodes data using printable characters; a MIME reader decodes the message.

modem (Modulator/DEModulator)

A device that encodes digital information in a carrier wave for transmission across copper wires or a dialup telephone connection. A pair of modems permits two-way communication because each modem contains circuitry to encode outgoing data and decode incoming data. See DSU/CSU.

modulation

The process of changing a carrier wave (usually a sine wave) to encode information. The frequency of the carrier and the modulation technique determine the rate at which data can be sent.

MTU (Maximum Transmission Unit)

The largest amount of data that can be sent across a given network in a single packet. Each network technology defines an MTU (e.g., the MTU of an Ethernet is 1500 octets).

multicast

A form of addressing in which a set of computers is assigned one address; a copy of any datagram sew to the address is delivered to each of the computers in the set. Often used for audio or video conferences. See broadcast, cluster, and unicast.

multihomed

Any host computer that attaches to more than one network. In most protocol systems, a multihomed computer has more than one address.

multiplex

A general concept that refers to combining independent sources of information into a form that can be transmitted over a single communication channel. Multiplexing can occur both in hardware (i.e., electrical signals can be multiplexed) and in software (i.e., protocol software can accept messages sent by multiple application programs and send them over a single network to different destinations). See demultiplex:

Netware

The name of a network system developed and sold by Novell Incorporated.

network adapter

Synonym for a NIC.

network analyzer

A device that listens to a network, usually a LAN, in promiscuous mode and reports on traffic. Also called a network monitor.

network management

A reference to the job of administering, monitoring, and controlling a network. Protocols like SNMP automate some of the monitoring and control tasks.

network monitor

A synonym for network analyzer.

next header

A field in an IPv6 header that specifies the type of the next item.

next-hop forwarding

The technique used by protocols like IP to forward a packet to its final destination. Although a given router does not contain complete information about the path a datagram will follow, the router does know the next router to which the datagram should be sent.

NFS (Network File System)

A remote file access mechanism originally defined by Sun Microsystems for use with the UNIX operating system. NFS allows applications on one computer to access files on a remote computer.

NIC (Network Interface Card)

A hardware device that plugs into a computer and connects the computer to a network. Often called a network adapter.

node

A term used informally to refer to a router or a computer attached to a network. The term is derived from graph theory.

Nyquist sampling theorem

An important result from information theory that specifies the number of samples that must be taken to digitize and then reconstruct a wave. The sampling theorem applies to sending audio over a network. See Shannon's Theorem.

OC (Optical Carrier)

A set of standards adopted by common carriers for the high-speed transmission of digital information over optical fiber. OC-1 operates at 51.840 Mbps; *OC-n* runs at *n* times that bit rate. See STS.

OC-3 (Optical Carrier 3)

A standard for the optical fiber encoding used in popular telephone company digital circuits. An OC-3 circuit operates at 155.520 Mbps. See OC.

odd parity

A parity bit added to a unit of data, usually each character, to make the number of/bits odd. A receiver checks the parity to determine whether data has been corrupted during transmission. See even parity.

optical fiber

Glass fiber used in computer networks. The chief advantage of optical fiber over copper wire is that fiber supports higher bandwidth. See fiber modem.

optical modem

A synonym for fiber modem.

OUI (Organizationally Unique Identifier)

A field in an LLC header that specifies which organization assigned the numbers used for type information.

packet

A small, self-contained parcel of data sent across a computer network. Each packet contains a header that identifies the sender and recipient, and data to be delivered.

packet switching network

Any communication network that accepts and delivers individual packets of information. Most modem networks are packet switching.

PAR (Positive Acknowledgement with Retransmission)

The basic technique protocols use to achieve reliable delivery. The receiving protocol returns an acknowledgement when a packet arrives. After transmitting a packet, the sender starts a timer. If the acknowledgement does not arrive before the timer expires, the sender retransmits the packet.

parity bit

An extra bit added to a unit of data, usually each character, to verify that the data is transferred without corruption. A receiver checks the parity on each incoming unit of data. See even parity and odd parity.

path MTU

The maximum amount of data that can be sent along the path from a source to a destination in one packet. Technically, the MTU of a path is the minimum MTU of any network along the path.

payfoad

Generically, the data being carried in a packet. The payload of a frame is the data in the frame; the payload of a datagram is the data area of the datagram.

PCM (Pulse Code Modulation)

The technique used to sample audio and encode it for transmission across a telephone network. PCM uses 8000 samples per second, with each sample encoded in 8 bits.

phase shift

A technique modems use to modulate a carrier. The phase of the carrier wave is shifted to encode data.

physical address

A synonym for hardware address.

ping (packet inter-net groper)

A program used to test network connectivity. Ping sends an ICMP Echo Request message to a destination, and reports whether it receives an ICMP Echo Reply as expected.

plug-and-play networking

Characteristic of any network system that allows a new computer to begin communicating without requiring configuration by the network manager. DHCP provides plug-and-play internet connections.

point-to-point network

Any network technology that uses a non-shared technology to connect pairs of computers. Point-to-point technology is more popular in Wide Area Networks than in Local Area Networks.

PRI (Primary Rate Interface)

An ISDN service that has sufficient bandwidth for larger businesses. See BRI.

propagation delay

The time required to send a signal across a network. The term comes from electrical engineering terminology, and describes an electrical signal propagating down a wire.

promiscuous mode

A mode in which a computer connected to a shared network captures all packets, including packets destined for other computers. Promiscuous mode is useful for network monitoring, but presents a security risk for a production network. Many standard interfaces allow promiscuous mode.

protocol

A design that specifies the details of how computers interact, including the format of messages they exchange and how errors are handled. See protocol suite.

protocol address

A number assigned to a computer that is used as the destination address in packets sent to that computer. Each IP address is 32 bits long; other protocol families use other sizes of protocol addresses.

protocol configuration

A step that a computer system must perform to assign values to parameters before protocol software can be used. Usually, protocol configuration requires a system to obtain a protocol address.

protocol port number

A small integer used to identify a specific application program on a remote computer. Transport protocols like TCP assign a unique port number to each service (e.g., e-mail uses port 25).

protocol suite

A set of protocols that work together to provide a seamless communication system. Each protocol handles a subset of all possible details. The Internet uses the TCP/IP protocol suite. See stack.

PVC (Permanent Virtual Circuit)

A connection from one computer to another through a connection-oriented network. A PVC is permanent in the sense that it survives computer reboots or power cycles; a PVC is virtual because it is achieved by placing routes in routing tables, not by establishing physical wires. See SVC.

queuing delay

The total amount of time a packet must wait in packet switches as it travels through a packet switching network. The queueing delay is related to the amount of traffic in a network—when no other packets are being sent, the queueing delay is zero.

RARP (Reverse Address Resolution Protocol)

A protocol that a computer system uses during bootstrap to obtain an IP address.

reassembly

The procedure a receiver uses to recreate a copy of an original datagram from the fragments that arrive. See fragmentation.

redirect

An ICMP error message sent from a router to a host. The message specifies that the host has an incorrect route which should be changed, and specifies the destination and a correct next-hop to reach that destination.

replay

A condition in which the arrival of a copy of an old packet confuses communication. For example, if a copy of a packet that requests termination of a communication is delayed until after a new communication has begun, the packet can incorrectly cause termination of the new communication. Protocols must be designed to prevent replay from causing problems.

retransmission

The retransmission of a packet that has been sent previously. Transport protocols use retransmission to achieve reliability. See PAR.

RF (Radio Frequency)

A range of frequencies used for sending radio signals through the air (e.g., from a commercial radio station). Wireless network technologies use RF.

RF modem

A modem that can send and receive information by modulating a radio frequency carrier. RF modems are used in wireless network technologies.

ring topology

A network architecture in which computers are linked into a cycle with the first connected lo the second, the second connected to the third, and so on until the last connects back to the first. Ring topology is usually used in Local Area Networks.

RJ-45

The type of connector used with twisted pair Ethernet.

root server

A domain name server that knows the locations of top-level domains such as *.com* and *edu.* See DNS and domain.

router

The bask building block of an internet. A router is a computer that attaches to two or man networks and forwards packets according to information found in its routing table. Routers in the Internet run the IP protocol. See host.

routing table

A table used by routing software to determine the next hop for a packet. A routing table is kept in a router's memory.

RS-232-C

The technical name of the standard used for serial data connections such as those between a keyboard and a computer. The standard defines such details as the voltage used to represent a/and a *0*.

segment

A single piece of cable that forms a bus network. Multiple segments can be connected by bridges or routers. A hub simulates a single segment.

self-healing network

A network system that has the ability to automatically detect a hardware failure and route traffic along an alternative path. Self healing requires redundant paths. FDDI is the best known self healing network technology.

serial line

A physical wire between two points over which data is sent one bit at a time. RS-232-C is often used with serial lines.

server

When two programs communicate over a network, a client is the one that initiates communication, while the program that waits to be contacted is a server. A given program can act as a server for one service and a client for another.

Shannon's Theorem

An important result that specifies the maximum data rate that can be achieved over a transmission channel that has noise associated with it. See Nyquist's Theorem.

shielded twisted pair

A cable that contains one (or more) twisted pairs of wire surrounded by a heavy metal shield similar to the shield that surrounds a single wire in a coaxial cable. The shield protects the inner pairs of wires from electrical interference.

signal loss

The amount of electrical energy lost as a wave travels down a medium such as a copper wire. A network connection cannot be arbitrarily long because the signal loss eventually makes the wave too weak to detect.

sliding window

A technique that a protocol can use to improve throughput by allowing a sender to transmit additional packets before receiving any acknowledgement. A receiver tells a sender how many packets can be sent at one time (called a window size).

SMDS (Switched Multi-megabit Data Service)

A connectionless Wide Area Network technology offered by telephone companies.

SMTP (Simple Mail Transfer Service)

The protocol used to transfer e-mail from one computer to another across the Internet. SMTP is part of the TCP/IP protocol suite.

SNAP (SubNetwork Attachment Point)

Part of the IEEE LLC/SNAP header used to identify the type of a packet. The entire header is *8* octets, with the SNAP portion occupying the last five. See LLC.

sniffer

A synonym for network analyzer taken from a popular product.

SNMP (Simple Network Management Protocol)

The protocol that specifies how a network management station communicates with agent software in remote devices such as routers. SNMP defines the format of messages and their meaning. See MIB.

socket API

A set of procedures that an application program can use to communicate across a network. The name arises because the set includes a *socket* procedure that must be called to establish communication. See API.

source address

An address in a packet that specifies the computer that sent the packet In a hardware frame, the source address must be a hardware address. In an IP datagram, the source address must be an IP address.

SPF (Shortest Path First)

A general link-state algorithm that routers can use to compute routes. See link-state and distance-vector.

spread spectrum

A transmission technique used to avoid interference and achieve higher throughput. Instead of a single carrier frequency, a sender and receiver agree to use a set of frequencies, either at the same time or by changing from one to another. The technique is especially important for wireless networks.

stack

An informal term for an implementation of a protocol suite. The term arises because a protocol layering diagram shows protocols in a vertical "stack".

star topology

A network architecture that consists of a central hub to which all computers connect. Star topologies are often used with Local Area Networks (e.g., twisted pair Ethernet). See hub and switch.

static document

A page of information available on the World Wide Web. The contents of a static document do not change until the author places new information in the document. See active document, dynamic document, and URL.

store and forward

Characteristic of a network that uses packet switches to forward packets. The name arises because each switch along a path to the destination receives a packet and temporarily stores the packet in memory. Meanwhile the switch continuously selects a packet from the queue in memory, routes the packet, and then transmits the packet to the appropriate next hop.

STS (Synchronous Transport Signal)

A set of standards adopted by common carriers for high-speed digital circuits. STS-1 operates at 51.840 Mbps: STS-n runs at *n* times that bit rate. See OC.

subnet mask

A synonym for address mask.

suite

See protocol suite.

SVC (Switched Virtual Circuit)

A connection from one computer to another through a connection-oriented network. An SVC is virtual because it is achieved by placing routes in routing tables, not by establishing physical wires; an SVC is switched because it can be created on demand analogous to a telephone call. See PVC.

switch

An electronic device that forms the center of a star topology network. A switch uses the destination address in a frame to determine which computer should receive the frame.

switching

A general term used to describe the operation of a switch. Because it is associated with hardware, switching is usually higher speed than routing. Also, switching differs from routing because switching uses the hardware address in a frame.

synchronous

Characteristic of any communication system in which the sender must coordinate (i.e., synchronize) with the receiver before sending data. Synchronization is usually handled by having the sending hardware transmit a regular pulse when no data is available. The receiver uses the pulses to extract data from the incoming signal. See asynchronous.

T1.T3

The designations that telephone companies use for popular point-to-point digital circuits. A T_1 circuit operates at 1.544 Mbps and a T3 circuit operates at 44.736 Mbps. See DS-l, DS-3.

TCP (Transmission Control Protocol)

The TCP/IP protocol that provides application programs with access to a connection-oriented communication service. TCP offers reliable, flow-controlled delivery. More important TCP accommodates changing conditions in the Internet by adapting its retransmission scheme. See UDP.

TCP/IP

The protocol suite used in the Internet. Although the suite contains many protocols, TCP and IP are two of the most important.

terminator

A device attached to the end of a wire or a transmission cable to prevent electrical signals from reflecting back. A bus network such as an Ethernet requires each end of the cable to have a terminator.

TFTP (Trivial File Transfer Protocol)

A protocol used to transfer a file from one computer to another. TFTP is simpler than FTP. but does not have as much capability.

thick wire Ethernet

An informal term used for the original DIX Ethernet.

Thicknet

A synonym for thick wire Ethernet.

thin wire Ethernet

An informal term used for the version of Ethernet that uses thinner coaxial cable.

Thinnet

A synonym for thin wire Ethernet.

time division multiplexing

A general multiplexing technique that allows multiple senders to transmit across a common medium. The senders take turns using the medium.

token passing

A technique used in ring topology networks to control transmission. The token consists of a special message sent around the ring. When a station has a packet to send, the station waits for the token to arrive, sends one packet, and then sends the token.

token ring

A ring topology network that uses token passing for access control. The phrase also applies to a specific token passing ring topology defined by IBM Corporation.

topology

A term used to describe the general shape of a network. Common topologies include bus.ring. star, and point-to-point.

TP Ethernet (Twisted Pair Ethernet)

See lOBase-T.

transceiver

An electronic device that connects the Network Interface Card in a computer to a physical medium. Transceivers are used with thick wire Ethernet.

transmission error

Any change introduced as data passes across a network. Transmission errors can be caused by electrical interference or hardware that malfunctions.

trunk circuit

A term with more than one meaning. Telephone companies use the term to refer to large-capacity circuits that form the main interconnect of the phone network (e.g., between cities). Cable television companies use the term to refer to the high-capacity coaxial cables used to connect between the cable company and neighborhood concentration points, which can be up to fifteen miles long. See feeder circuit.

twisted pair

A form of wiring in which a pair of wires is wrapped around one another again and again. Twisting two wires reduces their susceptibility to electrical interference.

UDP (User Datagram Protocol)

The TCP/IP protocol that provides application programs with connectionless communication service. See TCP.

unicast

A form of packet delivery in which each computer is assigned a unique address. When a packet is sent to a unicast address, exactly one copy of the packet is delivered to the computer to which the address corresponds. Unicast delivery is the most common type. See broadcast, cluster, and multicast.

URL (Uniform Resource Locator)

A syntactic form used to identify a page of information on the World Wide Web.

VC (virtual circuit)

A connection from one computer to another through a connection-oriented network. The term *virtual* arises because the circuit is achieved by placing routes in routing tables, not by establishing physical wires. Also called a virtual channel.

vector-distance

The original name for distance-vector.

virtual channel

A synonym for virtual circuit. The term virtual channel is used with technologies such as ATM. See VC.

WAN (Wide Area Network)

A network that uses technology designed to span a large geographic area. For example, a satellite network is a WAN because a satellite can relay communication across an entire continent. WANs have higher propagation delay than LANs. See LAN.

Web

A synonym for World Wide Web.

window

An amount of data that a receiver is willing to accept at any time. Window size can be measured in packets or in bytes. See sliding window.

WWW (World Wide Web)

The hypermedia system used on the Internet in which a page of information can contain text, images, audio or video clips, and references to other pages. See active document, dynamic document, static document, URL and browser.

xDSL (Digital Subscriber Line)

A generic acronym used to refer to any to the local loop technologies such as ADSL, HDSL, etc.

zero compression

A technique IPv6 uses to abbreviate hexadecimal colon notation by replacing a sequence of zeroes with a pair of colons.

Bibliography

Aiyer, S.S. Management of education: Efficiency of Computer-based Training, *Proceedings of Seminar on International Training and Development Conference,* New Delhi, (1987) pp. 28-29.

Distributed Multimedia Digital Libraries for Medical Education.

Gerhard Weikam, *Quality of Service guarantees for Multimedia Libraries and Beyond.* http://www-dbs.cs.uni-sb.de/ http://www.cs.purdue.edu/vdbms/papers/medlib.

Harrod, L.M., *Librarian's Glossary and Reference Book.* Boulder, Colo.: Westview Press. Rev. ed. 44.

IT Action Plan, July 4, 1998 by National Task Force on IT and Software Development, Government of India, 231-33.

Ian Gortan, *Essential Software Architecture,* National ICT, Australia, Springer Publications.

Khurana, R., Emerging Trends in Educational and Training Methodologies, including Satellite-based Techniques, Interactive Techniques, Technical Support for Learning. Seminar-*cum*-Workshop on Systems Approach to Training and Modern Instructional Techniques. *Military College of Telecommunications Engineering. Mhow (M.P.),* September 23, 1997.

Leider. Dorothy E. The use of IT to Enhance Management School Education: A Theoretical View, *MIS Quarterly,* September 1995, 62-64.

Prashant Praveen, *Technology and Management Education Delivery,* best student paper Competition of Association of Indian Management School, 1997, pp. 26-29.

Rawlings, B., New Technology—New Problem: The Knowledge Gap between Management and Computing. *The New Management Challenges*, 1988.

Ramaiah, C.K., Multimedia Systems in Libraries and their Applications. *DESIDOC Bulletin of IT 1998*, pp. 25-35.

Satyanarayana, B., Ramesh Babu and Pulla Reddy, Ashok Babu, eds. (1998) *Information Technology: Issues and Trends*, Delhi: Cosmo Publications.

Scheme for Computer Application Paper at Post-graduate Level in Certain Disciplines—UGC Assistance therefore, *Guidelines for Courses in Emerging Areas.... UGC*, New Delhi, 1993, pp. 329-30.

Index